George Rutledge Gibson

The stock exchanges of London, Paris, and New York

A comparison

George Rutledge Gibson

The stock exchanges of London, Paris, and New York
A comparison

ISBN/EAN: 9783337110352

Printed in Europe, USA, Canada, Australia, Japan

Cover: Foto ©Suzi / pixelio.de

More available books at **www.hansebooks.com**

THE STOCK EXCHANGES

OF

LONDON, PARIS, AND NEW YORK

A COMPARISON

BY

GEORGE RUTLEDGE GIBSON

NEW YORK & LONDON
G. P. PUTNAM'S SONS
The Knickerbocker Press
1889

COPYRIGHT BY
GEORGE RUTLEDGE GIBSON
1888

Press of
G. P. Putnam's Sons
New York

The warlike power of every country depends on their Three per Cents. If Cæsar were to reappear upon earth Wettenhall's (Stock Exchange) List would be more important than his Commentaries; Rothschild would open and shut the temple of Janus; Thomas Baring, or Bates, would probably command the Tenth Legion, and the soldiers would march to battle with loud cries of Scrip and Omnium reduced, Consols and Cæsar.—SYDNEY SMITH.

CONTENTS.

CHAPTER	PAGE
I.—THE STOCK EXCHANGE AS A FACTOR IN POLITICAL ECONOMY	1
II.—SPECULATION	6
III.—LONDON—THE ORIGIN OF THE PUBLIC DEBT AND THE STOCK EXCHANGE	15
IV.—LONDON—THE MODERN STOCK EXCHANGE,	22
V.—LONDON—THE MODERN STOCK EXCHANGE (*Continued*)	29
VI.—LONDON—TRADING "FOR THE ACCOUNT" AND CLEARING HOUSE FOR SHARES IN THE STOCK EXCHANGE	37
VII.—PARIS—THE BOURSE: ITS ORIGIN AND GROWTH	50
VIII.—PARIS—THE BOURSE—PARQUET AND COULISSE.	58
IX.—NEW YORK—EARLY HISTORY OF THE STOCK EXCHANGE	67
X.—NEW YORK—THE STOCK EXCHANGE OF TO-DAY	73
XI.—NEW YORK—THE COMMANDING INFLUENCE OF THE STOCK EXCHANGE	85
XII.—TECHNICAL TERMS OF STOCK EXCHANGES,	95
XIII.—NEW YORK—THE CONSOLIDATED STOCK AND PETROLEUM EXCHANGE: ITS ORIGIN AND GROWTH	107
XIV.—NEW YORK—METHODS OF BUSINESS ON THE CONSOLIDATED EXCHANGE	114
XV.—THE SO-CALLED BUCKET-SHOPS	120

LIST OF ILLUSTRATIONS.

	PAGE
BANK OF ENGLAND	*Frontispiece*
STOCK EXCHANGE OF LONDON. CAPEL COURT	24
STOCK EXCHANGE OF LONDON. SHORTER'S COURT	30
STOCK EXCHANGE OF LONDON. INTERIOR	42
THE PARIS BOURSE	58
THE NEW YORK STOCK EXCHANGE. BROAD STREET	74
THE NEW YORK CONSOLIDATED EXCHANGE. BROADWAY	108

NOTE.—The publishers beg to state that they made an effort to secure from the authorities of the Stock Exchange of London permission to have made a photograph of the interior of the building. This permission was, however, refused, and they have therefore been compelled to use for their illustration an old print, the only view now extant, and which fortunately represents very nearly the appearance of the interior to-day.

CHAPTER I.

THE STOCK EXCHANGE AS A FACTOR IN POLITICAL ECONOMY.

WORKS on history and political economy are singularly deficient in the treatment of Stock-Exchange business, and in fact completely ignore its important relations to the financial mechanism. Literary publications rarely enter into the consideration of this topic, which is foreign to the thoughts and classical education of most authors. Financial journals address their articles to the relatively narrow circle which is familiar with stock-markets and financial affairs. It therefore happens that the Stock Exchange, which is a most potent factor in the financial world, and one which powerfully affects wide interests, is imperfectly understood. Doubtless there are many persons who regard the Stock Exchange merely as a noisy congregation of brokers who gamble in the securities of governments and joint-stock companies, under the guise of legitimate business. Deeper insight into the functions, practices, and character of the Stock Exchanges in the three great cities of London, Paris, and New York may induce a broader and happier conception of their dignity and utility.

It would not be hazarding much to say that those who teach political economy in our schools, or write treatises on it for publication, are seldom familiar with the operations of Stock Exchanges. It follows that, in discussing and wrangling over the question of the evils or advantages of an adverse "balance of trade" between nations, they are likely to consult chiefly the statistics of imports and exports of commodities, merchandise, and specie, without trying to trace the more elusive but very palpable movement of financial securities. The Stock Exchange is the *deus ex machina* in the drama of commerce.

During the first eight months of 1888, to illustrate, the balance of trade, commercially, was ninety-two million dollars against the United States, but during that time we exported only about twenty-two millions in specie, leaving seventy millions unaccounted for. We should have been compelled to ship this seventy millions in specie to settle the international account had not foreign capital purchased liberally of our railway bonds and stocks. The balance of trade is nominally always against England, but instead of losing wealth, as the figures might suggest, that country is constantly growing richer by returns on investments made long ago wherever commerce thrives. Unless the ebb and flow of securities between great financial centres be studied and traced, the figures of international trade balances may be misconstrued or, indeed, wholly misunderstood. Political economy has at best, hardly established itself on the safe basis of an incontrovertible science, and it cannot afford to omit the facts and figures of Stock Exchanges in making up its conclusions as to balances of trade, interest on capital, and the production and distribution of wealth.

As will be more fully brought out later, the Exchanges of the world are instruments of enormous economic value in subdividing capital and directing its employment in the great works of commerce and industry.

The United States has been a vast and prolific field for foreign capital, and English solicitude for and interest in American affairs

centres in the Stock Exchange of New York.
The American visiting Great Britain, on his
arrival at Queenstown or Southampton, eagerly
seizes the latest paper to see what has trans-
pired at home since he sailed on his voyage
thither. He finds, perchance, a brief paragraph
or two about a national political convention, a
strike among railway employés, or a severe
storm, with no news of American society, art,
or literature. There is one thing, however,
which he sees spread out in satisfactory
detail, and that is the market reports, especially
the quotations of railway securities. That is
what most interests our British cousins in
their "kin beyond the sea."

Per contra, when the Wall-Street man goes
down to his office his first inquiry is for the two-
o'clock prices on the Stock Exchange of London,
which, owing to the difference in time of five
hours, are received before ten o'clock in New
York.

The quotations of American stocks, with the
accompanying price of Consols and the Bank
of England rate, inform him of the temper of
European capital and the status of politics,
commerce, and credit abroad as translated into
figures by the keenest financiers, besides serving

as a guide to his judgment of values here. The largest private banking institutions in London, Paris, Berlin, Vienna, and New York, combine the functions of banking and brokerage in such intimate relations that it is hard to say where the one begins and the other ends. Between the extremes of a deposit, discount and exchange business, and that of buying and selling bonds and shares on the Stock Exchanges of the world on commission, they negotiate loans for governments and corporations, reorganize properties, convert them from private into joint stock ownership, and are intermediaries in all the great movements of capital from one country to another. The community of financial interest between Great Britain and the United States, in particular, is one of the most effective agents for the promotion of peace and good-will between the nations.

The electric current which courses along the Atlantic cable binds Capel Court and Wall Street into the brotherhood of capital as well as of kindred and speech.

CHAPTER II.

SPECULATION.

DURING the past century panics have recurred in cycles of about ten years, and many superficial observers attribute them wholly to unhealthy speculation or gambling, and condemn Stock Exchanges as breeding-places of disaster.

Now, this word "speculation" has a bad name, and it may be worth while to see what it really implies or describes. Evidences of public debt, and the shares, bonds, and debentures of incorporated or chartered companies are easily transferred, are actively dealt in on the Exchanges and frequently are footballs for speculation, especially before their values are well established. Risk and uncertainty are the two qualities essential to speculative transactions, and just so fast and so far as they are eliminated, just so fast and so far they cease to invite speculation. All must alike deplore the frequent instances where the haste to get rich in speculative markets has involved innocent persons in loss and ruin, or tempted men to betray their trusts. But "the evil is passing and the good remains."

While panics have injured the pride and purse of individuals, and for the moment prostrated the energies of the industrial world, they have not arrested the progress of material civilization, but, indeed, seem, in a measure, to be merely an outgrowth from it. The extension of the credit system, which is one of the refinements of modern commerce; the introduction of labor-saving machinery, which rapidly displaces labor and deranges values, are two of the potent causes of commercial crises. The subdivision of the title of ownership of such great engines of progress as manufacturing, shipping, mining, banking, trading, telephone, telegraph, cable, water, and gas companies, is indispensable to their organization and operation. The fortune of no individual would be ample to set these forces into motion on a gigantic scale. As an illustration, the small streams of isolated and unused capital which trickle into the savings-banks of California, are returned in the waters of an irrigating canal which wash out the auriferous gravel or convert into gardens the sandy

desert. The Stock Exchanges of the world offer a
standing reward to men of talent and ingenuity
everywhere, to discover new opportunities and
to suggest untried experiments for the employment of capital, with a prospect of more than
an investor's rate of interest.

Not long ago steam was applied to locomotion
by land and sea, and electricity to the transmis-
sion of thought and speech. Their introduction
was an experiment; they were at first a speculation, and not an investment. Speculation is
truly the handmaid of enterprise, and the two
are so closely associated that one cannot be cur-
tailed without crippling the other.

The person who buys more shares than his
capital will permit him to pay for, is derisively
called a "speculator." But does this act essentially differ from the practices of what, by common consent, are called legitimate commercial un-
dertakings? The merchant buys in advance of
his immediate wants and in excess of them and
of his capital. The real-estate owner pledges his
property to procure money to improve it or
to buy more, expecting to sell at a profit. But
the critic here says: "On the Stock Exchange
speculators go so far as to sell what they do
not possess," or in Stock-Exchange parlance

they "go short." But how about the contractor who agrees to build a house before he owns a plank, or brick, or nail; or who agrees to build a railway before he buys a cross-tie, a rail, or a shovel? How about the manufacturer who sells his sheetings and his steel rails, before the cotton is grown or the ore extracted from the mine? Even China, our commercial antipodes, sells its products to us ahead of their production. The fact is, that the element of speculation constantly comes more prominently into the plans of the whole mercantile world. Those who produce or buy only what they need from day to day, jog along as did the canal boats and stage coaches of our ancestors. The great manufacturers and merchants of to-day must cast the horoscope of coming conditions and read its prophecy aright or be overcome by more prescient rivals. They must anticipate and discount the future, and become speculators in the highest acceptation of the word.

As the current of progress rolls on, innocent persons are occasionally caught in the eddies, and others are engulfed in the whirlpool rapids of speculation; but the stream of prosperity flows steadily on.

As steam is explosive, electricity deadly; as

tuberculosis lurks in milk, typhoid fever in water, and trichinæ in meat, so the stock-market is full of manholes and pitfalls. It is equally true that statistics disclose the lamentable fact that 95 per cent. of all business men fail at some period of their lives. All kinds of grist come to the mill, and since it requires an infallible judgment invariably to detect the chaff of fraud and folly, all classes are alike exposed to peril in business. Financial storms may manifest themselves with a greater cyclonic fury within the precincts of the Stock Exchange, but they are equally destructive in commercial and industrial circles. Bonds and shares are the most mercurial and sensitive forms which capital assumes, but as a sudden wave of heat registers its arrival more quickly on a bulb of mercury than on a bar of iron, so the former more quickly recovers its normal temperature. It is so with Stock-Exchange markets, which are first to feel a financial barometic depression, but likewise the first to record a better atmosphere, while real estate, for instance, is the last to detect, as well as the last to recover.

The Stock Exchange and banks of the large cities are closely allied, and together constitute the money-market. Banks cluster about the

Stock Exchange, for bonds and shares are among the most desirable collateral securities for loans, and the testimony of bankers would easily be that losses from this source show a much smaller percentage than in commercial paper.

The value of shares is distinctly enhanced by "listing" them, as Wall Street would say, or by "granting a quotation," in the language of Capel Court. With law supreme, paper titles to property are as secure as its personal possession, and when these shares become publicly known in an open market, the value which they there acquire may be regarded as the judgment of the best intelligence concerning them. If there is merit, it becomes known to more people with capital than if the property be merely held in private ownership, or dealt in outside the Exchange. Thus we see that a railway, a brewery, a bank, a piece of land, or a mine is mobilized, so to speak, and acquires greater negotiability on its introduction to an Exchange, the arena of speculation. The banker will loan more money on it, and more people will buy in it, because there is always a ready market in case they wish to change that investment. Here is where the Stock Exchange does a good service to capital, and this is why its existence is a constant incentive to promoters, inventors, and men of original and progressive ideas.

Every occurrence in the commercial world is communicated to its nerve-centres—the Stock Exchanges,—where the importance or bearings of the event are at once estimated. In earlier days, carrier-pigeons, or private expresses in post haste brought to the stock-market the news which now is borne by the electric telegraph. Brokers and speculators vie with each other for the fastest means of procuring and transmitting information. Representatives of brokers, in times of critical interest, follow armies in the field, shadow diplomats, sit in legislative halls, visit mines, workshops, and farms, each eager to procure advance information. A silver bill in Washington, a railway strike in the Northwest, a war of rates between trunk lines, yellow fever in Florida, a bank failure in San Francisco, a revolution in Mexico, floods in Hungary, a drought in India, a panic in Buenos Ayres, an advance in the Bank-of-England rate, a peaceful speech by the Prime-Minister, a riot in the streets of Paris, an inflammatory article in a St. Petersburgh paper, the death of an Emperor in Germany, the imposition of a new tariff in Austria, the success of a large loan in

Amsterdam, and so on *ad infinitum;* all are
noted in the Exchanges of the world, and some
interests are correspondingly influenced upon receipt of the news. There are three news agencies
in New York whose duties are to collect and
distribute just such information as this, and
brokers before whom it is laid are at once compelled to estimate its correctness and value and
apply it instantly to the stock-market. Rapidity
of reasoning and quickness of decision are the
two qualities most essential to the stock-broker
and stock-operator.

Many leading brokers, particularly in America, issue a printed daily, weekly, or monthly
résumé of the shifting phases of the market,
discussing its underlying conditions, as well as
surface indications. These letters go to their
clients, who are thus informed of the conclusions
of observers, who in their interest are seeking
to discover the hidden springs which move
prices and values. These productions are as
broad in their grasp as those of financial jour-
nalistic writers, and they have perhaps the ad-
vantage of being written by men who are in
close and constant touch with affairs. Narrow-
ness of view there may be by those who frequent
the Stock Exchange, but the broad horizon

which knows not the boundaries of race, empire, or religion, must be swept by the vision of those who would succeed there in a large way.

CHAPTER III.

LONDON—THE ORIGIN OF THE PUBLIC DEBT AND THE STOCK EXCHANGE.

LONDON, which holds the purse-strings of the world, is, of course, the seat of its most powerful Stock Exchange. While its beginnings are misty they are not remote, for only well inside of two hundred years have there been any opportunities for the exercise of a stock-broker's vocation.

William III. was the founder of the English debt, of the Bank of England (1694), and of national fiscal honor. Charles I. had seized the gold deposited in the Mint. Charles II. had closed the Exchequer, confiscating one million three hundred thousand pounds sterling, and as Hallam says, "The nation had sunk to the nadir of its prosperity." William acknowledged the debt so infamously incurred and repudiated by his predecessors, and thereafter paid an annual interest upon it. While the government was thus learning the secret of extracting money from the people by lawful methods, and sowing the seed of the great harvest of modern national debt, merchants were discovering the advantages of exclusive charters for commercial enterprises. By purchase or by royal favor the East India, the Hudson Bay, and other companies established themselves in monopolies in the 17th century, and became the forerunners of that host of trading companies which pushed English commerce into the remotest corners of the globe. With the establishment of the public debt and national integrity, and the successful introduction of these great commercial organizations, the stock-broker makes his first appearance on the stage of English history.

There follows a period between 1716 and 1720 when England and France became a prey to a speculative mania, which is unexampled in financial history. The celebrated Mississippi scheme in France and the South Sea Bubble in England were the most extraordinary delusions that credulous cupidity ever produced. The imagination of all classes from lords to lackeys was captivated by a financial necromancy as extravagant as the professed magic of the philosopher's stone. "*Auri sacra fames*," the accursed thirst for gold, is a passion of the race and has been inseparable from human life in all its varying phases of intelligence. The dreams of avarice made a slave of the intelligence and judgment of men, and the shares of bubble companies rose with fatal celerity to a fatal height. When the rude awakening came the whole financial fabric crumbled in one common ruin. But the infatuation of the people and its sad denouement taught a lesson to the commercial world which thereafter led to greater prudence and exacter methods. Business is not a mathematical science, but experience teaches lessons in finance as in every thing else.

Parliament in 1720 passed an act prohibiting the formation of companies except by special charter, and this law was not repealed until 1826.

Stock-brokers and Stock Exchanges, as we know them to-day, are very different from their prototypes two hundred years ago, but all professions have alike emerged from the crudities and imperfections of an earlier time. The Royal Exchange, which was erected during the reign of Elizabeth, as a meeting-place for merchants, was the original rendezvous of the first stock-brokers. After a few years, or in 1698, the dealers in shares abandoned the Royal Exchange and took up their abode in Change Alley, a locality which they made famous. In those days coffee-houses were the trysting-places for social, political, and financial coteries, and Jonathan's and Garraways' in Change Alley became the home of the stock-brokers. In 1701 they were not esteemed as the most useful members of the community, as may be inferred from the criticism of a contemporary writer. He said: "They can ruin men silently, undermine and impoverish, fiddle them out of their money by the strange, unheard-of engines of interest, discount, transfers, tallies, debentures, shares, projects, and the devil and all of figures and hard names." Thomas Guy, the founder of Guy's Hospital, was one of those who amassed a fortune in the transactions which are thus so vehemently condemned.

The records of the Stock Exchange now in its archives do not go back of 1798, but it appears from outside sources that in Change Alley there was no organization, it being merely a common meeting-place without any restrictions or limitations whatever. About 1773 the scene shifted to the The Stock Exchange Coffee-House, Threadneedle Street, where a sixpence was charged for admission, though the Bank of England set aside the rotunda of the Bank for dealings in shares, debentures, and public funds, where a large traffic, for a time, was carried on.

During the latter part of the eighteenth, and the early part of the nineteenth centuries, the public debt was swollen by the American and Napoleonic wars, and the subsidies paid so freely by Pitt to foreign states. In 1775, at the commencement of the American Revolution, the British debt was £126,842,811, and in 1815, at the end of the French and American wars, the debt stood at £861,039,049. The price of Consols fluctuated violently in those days, rising from 57 in 1784 to 97 in 1792, declining to $47\frac{1}{4}$ in 1798. In 1802 they were 79, in 1803 $50\frac{1}{4}$, etc. From 1797 to 1819 specie payments were suspended, which added an element of speculation to business of all descriptions. In 1816, Bank-of-England notes showed as much as $16\frac{3}{4}$ per cent. discount, in gold. The increasing debt and wide variations in its market value naturally brought profit to brokers, whose business it was to buy and sell the public funds; besides, war always opens speculative opportunities. Therefore it is not surprising to learn that under this stimulus the Stock Exchange of London reached such a state of prosperity, and importance as to justify a new building. On May 18, 1801, the corner-stone of its present structure was laid in Capel Court, and in March, 1802, the Exchange, which then numbered 500 members, occupied its new quarters.

In the early part of the century Nathan Mayer Rothschild was one of the giants " on 'Change," and it was there he achieved his greatest triumphs after establishing the London house of Rothschild.

In those days the funds were subject to violent fluctuations, and the issue of peace or war, victory or defeat, was the decisive influence on values. This was before the era of telegraph and steam or the present systematic development of the postal and express service. Enterprise then involved personal fatigue and often heavy expense, but it was in this that lay much of Rothschild's success. One signal instance of this was his own personal journey to the field of Waterloo, where he felt the stakes were too great to justify his reliance on agents or couriers. He witnessed this battle of the Titans, saw that Napoleon was defeated, that the Allies had won, and instantly made his way to Brussels, thence by carriage to Ostend;

by bribing a hardy seaman with two thousand francs he secured a private passage to Dover in the midst of a tempest, and thence rode on to London, where, the following morning, looking most dejected, he stationed himself in his favorite place in the Stock Exchange. Brokers known often to represent him were open sellers of the funds, whilst he quietly bought heavily through others. He finally gave out the news, beating the government expresses and the speculative world, and amassed a handsome fortune out of this grand *coup*.

The annals of the Stock Exchange in those days are meagre, but they show that operators were exposed to hoaxes and canards of every description. False rumors are now often put into circulation to affect values, but the rapid means of communication in our time permit an immediate refutation and hence forbid serious injury.

CHAPTER IV.

LONDON—THE MODERN STOCK EXCHANGE.

AFTER the return of the disbanded armies of Europe to the pursuits of civil life, at the end of the Napoleonic wars, there was a revival of industry that amounted to its creation. The age of steam, electricity, and mechanical invention had dawned, and "swords were beaten into ploughshares, and knives into pruninghooks." Projects for the acquisition of wealth multiplied, but so many of them were visionary and impracticable that in 1826 a day of reckoning came. The panic of that year only cleared the decks for action, however, and it was not long before a fresh industrial movement was under way. This in its turn was arrested in 1836 in England, and in 1837 in the United States, only to be shortly renewed on an increasing scale. Ten years later the most remarkable period of speculative industrial enterprise of the century reached its climax in England, in what was commonly known as "the

The Modern Stock Exchange. 23

railway mania of 1845." The sums authorized to be expended by Acts of Parliament on railway enterprises were: in 1843, £3,861,285; in 1844, £17,870,361; in 1845, £60,824,088; in 1846, £160,026,224; in 1847, £40,397,395; in 1848, £14,620,471; in 1849, £3,155,332, or over £300,000,000 (say $1,500,000,000) in seven years.[1] Prior to 1844 one tenth of the estimated cost of a railway had to be deposited before the bill for its promotion could pass, but in that year this deposit was reduced to one twentieth.

At this juncture occurred the triumph of Cobden's principles, the conversion of the great Tory minister, Sir Robert Peel, the abolition of the Corn Laws, the Irish famine, succeeded by a panic in the spring of 1847. There had been a great drain of gold to purchase food supplies abroad, and the want of currency was so great that advances could not be obtained even on silver bullion. By some the crisis was attributed to the Bank Restriction Act of 1844, which prevented the Bank of England, with £9,000,000 in its vaults, from furnishing relief. In October, 1847, the operation of this act was suspended, and confidence was im-

[1] Francis's History of the Bank of England.

mediately restored. The speculative railway mania was responsible for some of the financial distress, but by no means for all of it. Next follows the panic of 1857, when specie payments in the United States and the Bank Act in England were suspended. In 1861 the United States was plunged into the great war of secession, causing another suspension of specie payments, but no general bankruptcy. In 1866 there occurred in England one of the worst panics of modern times, it being essentially a credit panic, as distinguished from the mercantile crises of 1847 and 1857. The rapid growth of the "limited-liability" companies under the laws of 1862 and previous years are charged with much of the mischief of this collapse. Great houses like Overend & Gurney, Morton, Peto, & Co., went down with a crash. The fall of securities on the Stock Exchange of London, as given on high authority, was one hundred million pounds sterling, and relief did not come until the Bank Act was again suspended. In 1873 the failure of Jay Cooke & Co., attended by widespread ruin in financial and industrial circles in America, and the panic in the spring of 1884, precipitated by the failure of the Marine Bank of New York City, are fresh in public memory, and need not be recounted.

STOCK EXCHANGE OF LONDON, CAPEL COURT.

These vicissitudes, and that host of unnamed events in England and abroad which have marked the growth of wealth during the past fifty years, greatly augmented speculative opportunities and expanded the volume of transactions to enormous proportions.

To-day the interests of the Stock Exchange are more varied and cosmopolitan than that of any other set of men in the world. If it has not bought and sold the earth, the title-deeds which have passed through its hands represent an empire of wealth, over which Crœsus would be too poor to preside.

The Bank of England is the apex of a vast pyramid of share capital, resting upon the broad basis of the world's commerce, and almost every atom of the mass is weighed, assayed, and a valuation stamped upon it by the Stock Exchange of London. The immense tide of traffic that beats up against the Bank of England, the Royal Exchange, and the Stock Exchange is but emblematic of England's commercial power. An observer has said that the sidewalks in that vicinity are "islands of retreat from the maelstrom of vehicles" which crowd this the busiest spot on the globe. The Bank, which covers an entire block and an area of three acres, in most part is only two stories in height, but in appearance it is the most substantial banking structure in any city, indeed a veritable fortification or Gibraltar of security. The Capel Court entrance to the Stock Exchange looks out upon the eastern front of the Bank, on Bartholomew Lane, but the other entrances on Throgmorton Street and Old Broad Street are more thronged. The Stock Exchange is not one of the "sights" of London, as its exterior is inconsequential and almost undistinguishable from contiguous buildings, and its interior is not open to public view. Unlike the Bourse in Paris, and the Stock Exchange in New York, there is no gallery for spectators. The building was wholly rebuilt in 1853, and has expanded to meet the increasing demands upon it, but with no well-defined architectural purpose, so that its blind passage-ways, winding stair-cases, and narrow closed doorways make it something of a puzzle to a stranger. The main room is octagonal in form, about 68 feet in diameter, with an iron and glass dome 110 feet in height from the floor to the top of the cupola. Its quarters are cramped, and it strikes an American that they ought to tear down the entire structure and erect one commensurate with the dignity and present requirements of the institution. There are, however, two obstacles to this: first, English preference for dinginess and the respectability of age, rather than spick-and-span architecture; and second, the nature of the ownership of the building. It belongs to a proprietary company, and not to the "House," as the general membership of the Exchange is denominated. Though only recently so, no one can be a shareholder in the company unless he be a member of the Exchange, but a person may be a member of the Exchange and not be a shareholder. The interests may not exactly conflict, but they are, to say the least, not identical, and it is a question if they be equitable. The annual dues of members range between twenty and thirty guineas, depending on the date of their admission; and the entrance fees of new members vary from £315 for an outsider to £131 5s. for those who have been clerks for four years. These payments all go to the proprietary company as a rental. This does not quite describe the fact, for the proprietary company appoint and pay all officials in charge of the building, and superintend it. This property is mortgaged to the extent of £240,000, bearing four-per-cent. interest, and the public may hold these debentures. The capital of the company is 20,000 shares paid up £12 each, and in the year 1886–7 they paid a dividend of £4 15s., or nearly 40 per cent. on the amount paid up. The entire property is now worth over five millions of dollars. The shares are owned by about one thousand persons, some of whom acquired them before the present restriction, which prevents persons not members of the Stock Exchange from becoming shareholders, was adopted.

CHAPTER V.

LONDON—THE MODERN STOCK EXCHANGE.

(*Continued*)

THE present membership of "The Stock Exchange of London" (its proper title) is about 2,850, which is double the number (1,433) in 1870. If the interests of shareholders and subscribers could in some way be amalgamated it would give a value to membership which would afford security to that extent to engagements between members, besides insuring a greater community of interest and more solidarity to the institution. There is no limit to membership, which may rise or fall, accordingly as business is found profitable or otherwise. In the Bourse at Paris and in the Exchanges of New York, memberships are fixed in number, and a candidate must procure a "seat" by purchase and transfer from a retiring member before he can be elected. In London, on the contrary, the applicant addresses the Secretary, announcing his wish to be admitted a member of the Stock Exchange for the year, commencing on the 25th of March, 18—, upon the terms of, and under and subject in all respects to the Rules and Regulations, etc. He further states: "I am a British subject and of age; I am (married or single); my residence is ——; my office is ——; my bankers are ——; I am not engaged in any business except such as is transacted at the Stock Exchange, nor am I a clerk in any public or private establishment unconnected with the Stock Exchange, nor a member of or subscriber to any other institution in which dealings in stocks or shares are carried on." Accompanying this is a document which reads: "We recommend Mr. —— as a fit person to be admitted a member of the Stock Exchange; and in case he shall be publicly declared a defaulter within four years from the date of his admission we, each of us, hereby engage to pay his creditors, upon application, the sum of five hundred pounds, to be applied in discharge of the said defaulter's debts in the Stock Exchange." This must be signed by three sponsors who have themselves been members for four years. Assuming them to be good, all those having dealings with the new member during the ensuing four years have

STOCK EXCHANGE OF LONDON, SHORTER'S COURT.
(Where American stocks are dealt in "after hours.")

an aggregate security of fifteen hundred pounds, but thereafter no security whatever, on account of his membership. If the applicant has for four years been a clerk in the Stock Exchange only two recommenders are required, to the extent of three hundred pounds each. No applicant is admissible if he be engaged as principal or clerk in any business other than that of the Stock Exchange, or if his wife be engaged in business. He must have been a citizen of Great Britain, either native or naturalized, for two years. The Committee of General Purposes, consisting of thirty members, is elected annually, and they elect from amongst themselves a Chairman, and Deputy-Chairman, and from the list of Stock-Exchange members they select a Secretary. Francis Levien, Esq., has for many years occupied this post with singular ability and fidelity. He is the repository of all the traditions, customs, practices, precedents, of the written and unwritten law and history of the Stock Exchange of London, in the same sense that Geo. W. Ely, Esq., Secretary of the New York Stock Exchange, and Charles G. Wilson, President of the Consolidated Stock Exchange of New York, are the authority on all such questions in New York. It usually happens that every large institution annually returns to office some one who is regarded as an encyclopædia of general information on its affairs.

The "Committee for General Purposes" in the Stock Exchange of London *annually re-elect the entire list of members*, unless for good cause some one or more should fail to pass. This feature is peculiar, but cannot be too strongly commended. It is a power subject, of course, to abuse by a member of the Committee exercising his influence to defeat a perfectly worthy candidate, but happily the malice of individuals does not often prevail. High character and inflexible rectitude among members is necessary to inspire and merit public confidence, and they are also indispensable in the inter-relations of members. It must be remembered that enormous transactions in all Exchanges are entered into in the most hurried manner, frequently closed by a nod or gesticulation, without written contract, witnesses, notarial acknowledgement, or calm comparison, and in the din and confusion of excited markets. Transactions are based absolutely on the confidence of man in man, and the power of discipline possessed by this London Committee is salutary, even though necessity seldom requires its exercise. There is a provision in the Stock Exchange of London, which is similar to the Bourse in Paris, but quite unlike the Exchanges in New York, whereby authorized clerks may be admitted, with power to deal and bind their principals, and unauthorized clerks, with merely the privilege of assisting their employers. A list of clerks is posted with the names of their employers, and this can be referred to at pleasure. There are also a number of members of the Exchange who are employed as clerks by other members, but so long as they are in the service of their fellow-members they are prohibited from doing any business in their own name or account.

One of the marked peculiarities of the Stock Exchange of London is the distinction between those who act as agents for the public, and who are technically called "brokers," and those who do business on their own account, and are described as "dealers" or "jobbers." It is estimated that about one third of the entire membership are brokers, one third dealers, and one third clerks to other members. The custom of the Exchange forbids any member from acting in the double capacity of broker and jobber, and prohibits partnerships between the two classes, and also with any person not a member of the Exchange. In the Bourse at Paris, all *agents de Change* are strictly forbidden to trade on their own account. In the Stock Exchanges of New York there is a large class of members who operate for their own account. They are called " room-traders " or " scalpers," whose profits or losses consist in quick turns made during the day, the interest that they have overnight, or over Sunday, being usually very small. They endeavor to detect the momentary influences and run of orders " going short " or " buying long " without reference to what they may think the ultimate course of prices will be. In New York, room-traders sometimes have orders to execute for friends, though they do not court that kind of business. Commission brokers in New York may occasionally trade on their own account, no regulations preventing it, and all members alike join in the groups assigned to different active stocks in making a market by open bids and offers.

In the Stock Exchange of London, however, "dealers" are by custom required to make a price at which they will buy and another at which they will sell, so that if a broker there receives a commission from his client to buy Lake Shore shares, for instance, he asks a dealer for the quotation. If he replies 96-96¼, that means that he will pay 96 or sell at 96¼ to the extent of one hundred shares, which is the rule in American shares. In British railways ten shares is the unit, and it may here be said that all shares to be a proper delivery in London must be in ten-share certificates. The bulk of the business is done in this way, and brokers as a rule buy from and sell to dealers of established reputation rather than with each other. This does not permit the free market we have in New York, nor the same closeness of price that is made here, where stocks can frequently be bought and sold in large amounts at the same price. Here a record is kept of the transactions, the stock list each day, showing pretty closely the number of shares traded in. In London and Paris these lists do not indicate the volume of business, merely giving quotations as they may be marked by brokers, on a public bulletin hanging in the Exchange, and consequently not accurate indices of the course and scope of the market. In both those markets, particularly in London, there is a secrecy and a disposition to conceal operations, which is a striking contrast with the frank and public manner of conducting the business in the

United States. Why members of the Stock Exchange should not be merged into a homogeneous mass, and why their operations should not be conducted on the principle of an auction, are not apparent to an American.

The Bourse in Paris and the Stock Exchange in London have a horror of printer's ink and publicity, which expresses itself in their rule forbidding members to advertise. The result of this is that irregular brokers and what in this country are called "bucket shops" advertise and no doubt secure commissions that would go to members of the Stock Exchange if they were permitted to solicit business. Prior to 1886 the City of London required all brokers to take out a license, and the result was persons outside of the Stock Exchange posed before the public as licensed brokers. The semi-official endorsement of the Corporation of London proved to be misleading to the public, and the law was repealed. The Secretary of the Stock Exchange publishes a notice in the daily papers warning the public that members of the Exchange are not allowed to advertise.

CHAPTER VI.

LONDON—TRADING "FOR THE ACCOUNT" AND CLEARING HOUSE FOR SHARES IN THE STOCK EXCHANGE.

BEFORE any scrip, shares, bonds, or debentures of any description can be quoted in the official lists, or be in any manner recognized by the Exchange, application must be made in behalf of such issues, and the proper committee will require full information as to the bona-fide character of the enterprise; that it is of sufficient magnitude to warrant dealings, that two thirds of the whole nominal capital have been applied for and unconditionally allotted to the public; that its issues are legal in form and authority, etc. It is *apropos* to remark that Stock Exchanges guard the public, in so far as they are able, in declining to admit to quotations the questionable enterprises of "shady" promoters, but they do not in any manner thereby indicate any opinion, personal or official, as to the value of such issues, or

their real genuineness or soundness. That is
entirely beyond their province, and persons
buying issues that have been "listed" should
scrutinize the property and investigate the
value for themselves. *Caveat emptor.* The
immense number of shares, stocks, bonds, debentures, etc., that are dealt in on the Stock
Exchange in London, as may be surmised, necessitates a systematic division of the scant
space in the Board Room. A portion of "the
floor" is given up to Consols, bank shares,
Indian securities, one to home railways, one to
the funds of foreign states; a department, and a
large one, to American railways, etc. The section of the floor assigned to these various interests are again subdivided into groups varying in
size with the activity and popularity of the different securities.

When a member wishes to obtain what he
purchases without delay, he stipulates at the
moment of negotiation that it is to be a cash
transaction, otherwise he would not receive
the certificates of ownership until the next
"settling day." These settling days are once
a month, in Consols, and twice a month,
about the middle and end, in all other securities. Practically, trading "for the account," as

Trading "for the Account." 39

this is called, is the mode in which nearly all the business is done, and under it purchases carry no interest during the current account, at the end of which the buyer receives the securities due him. If, before that day arrives, however, he should re-sell the same securities, there should in that case be no necessity for him to receive them from the person who sold to him, for him, in turn, to deliver to the person to whom he had sold. That would be superfluous labor and risk, and that he avoids by the intervention of a Clearing-House arrangement, which eliminates himself from the transaction by directing the ultimate seller to deliver to the ultimate buyer, the middle man receiving any difference in his favor, or paying any that is against him. This end is accomplished to some extent by passing around for endorsement a ticket, which is made to do duty as a settling agent, but the Clearing House is now as fixed and popular a factor in the Stock Exchange of London as among the banks of London and all other cities, in "clearing" or settling their differences. Many people have an idea that a Clearing House, by some necromantic power, transforms the ordinary business of the Exchanges into a speculative character. It does economize book-keeping, money, capital, risk of banks, and avoids the daily passing of stocks backward and forward through the streets like a shuttle, and perhaps the relief of the business from such burdens may promote activity and willingness to trade. But it is precisely as legitimate for brokers to adopt the economical agency of the Clearing House as for banks, who no longer cart their specie from one office to another. There are in London, for instance, twenty-seven banks belonging to the Bankers' Clearing House, and all other bankers in London and throughout England keep accounts with them. The Clearing-House banks all keep accounts in the Bank of England, and in the clearing of any day, debtor banks give their checks on the Bank of England, which the creditor banks deposit there, and thus not a sovereign passes, though, to illustrate, in the week ending July 4, 1888, £188,000,000 (nearly $950,000,000) were thus cleared. The principle of a Clearing House in its simplest form is where two men who are mutually indebted, instead of paying each debt in full, should "pair off," as far as the debts permit, the larger debtor then paying the excess. This same principle extends into international transactions, and the United States and England, instead of each shipping gold on all purchases in the other country, only do so to the extent of the balance of trade. When a dozen nations are trading together the Exchanges between them become more complex, but otherwise do not differ. It is with transactions between members of Stock Exchanges identically the same as between merchants of nations engaged in international commercial intercourse. Though this mode of settlement now obtains in English and Continental Exchanges, the Consolidated Exchange of New York, with a plan similar, but in some respects preferable, is the only Stock Exchange in the New World that adopts "trading for the account" with a Clearing House. The Stock Exchange of Philadelphia delivers stocks daily through the intervention of a Clearing House. In the Stock Exchange of London inactive securities, which are rarely dealt in, are not cleared, the list covering only such as are largely bought and sold.

All members of the Exchange are not necessarily registered in the Clearing House, and their participation in its operations is not compulsory. The Clearing House is of relatively recent origin in its application to stocks, in London, and at first some of the larger houses opposed its introduction as it to some degree destroyed their advantages over smaller brokers and dealers. They have, however, gradually come to acknowledge its vast superiority over the old system, and now the great bulk of the business goes through this mode of settlement. Members are gradually coming in, and the indications are that within a short time the entire membership will employ the Clearing House, which is conducted by the Exchange as a part of its official machinery. When the end of the fortnightly period arrives, three days are allowed to complete the settlement. The first is "Contango day," on which brokers and dealers balance their accounts to see what they have to deliver and what to receive as the net result of their operations for the preceding two weeks. Those who are "bull" of a certain stock must be prepared to receive the actual certificates upon the third day, which is called "settling day," the intervening one being known as "ticket day." The "bull" (French, *haussier*) must have the funds to pay for the securities, or he must borrow the money almost invariably on a pledge of collaterals from bankers or money-lenders, or he must arrange with the seller, the "bear" (French, *baissier*), or some

STOCK EXCHANGE OF LONDON—INTERIOR.

one else in the Exchange to have the stock carried over till the end of the next fortnightly period. If he pays for this extension, it is called a "contango" (French, *report*), which with us would be called interest or "carrying charge." If the seller is operating for "short" account, and finds it difficult to procure certificates to make the delivery, the buyer, to whom he owes stock, may only consent to forego for the next two weeks his right to receive it, for a consideration. The sum thus paid by the seller to defer the delivery is called "backwardation" (French, *déport*), which with us would be called a "premium." When the contract stands over till the next settlement without any interest or other charges either way, it is said to be "flat." All persons having arranged for the continuation into the next account of such contracts as are not to be settled by an actual delivery of the securities, and all offsetting contracts having been eliminated by the machinery of the Clearing House, "tickets" are exchanged between those members who have actual certificates to deliver, and on the third, or "settlement" day, these certificates are passed from the sellers to the buyers. Meanwhile trading goes on in the Exchange for the current account which in turn has its transactions subjected to the same process. No fixed commission is charged, but one eighth per cent. to buy and the same to sell is customary. Active speculative accounts when opened and closed during a fortnightly period are sometimes undertaken by responsible houses for one sixteenth each way. There is no place in the world where personal honor and credit, without security, go so far as in this Exchange. Contracts entered into "for the account" (French *à terme*) remain open until the date of the next settlement, and though a broker may have coming to him at that time an immense number of shares and bonds bought at lower prices, he has no power before that date to call upon the sellers to give any security whatever for the faithful performance of their contracts. A dealer might make engagements far beyond his ability, trusting that at the settlement period, or before, he might be able to repurchase stocks which he had sold short, or to sell stocks which he had bought, without disastrous loss, and if the market went against him he would meanwhile not be compelled to disclose his inability to make good the difference. An American cannot but regard this as an undue and unnecessary expansion of the credit system, and far inferior to the American plan in time contracts. The latter gives either party the right to demand a mutual deposit in any Trust Company (bank) of unexceptionable standing, or with the chairman of the Exchange, of ten per cent. of the amount involved in the open contract. This removes from American business an element of risk inherent in the English system. Americans have no conception of what " credit " means, for it is hedged about here by conditions and limitations unknown to brokers in London and Paris. The custom in London is to accept an uncertified check for securities passing between members of the Exchange; indeed the practice of certifying checks there is unknown. A member can, by giving proper notice, demand the actual cash, but that is only resorted to in desperate cases. In New York the common practice, especially in times of any uneasiness, of exacting a certified check, which is a check marked good by the bank on which it is drawn, for all sums of any magnitude, in lieu of the certificates or bonds delivered to the buyer, reduces the risk to a minimum, and is preferable to the English system, which all the way through is one of exceptional confidence.

No doubt the custom of granting credit there leads to a closer scrutiny of character, and as an aid to the proper estimate of the real status of a member is the rule forbidding him and his wife from being engaged in any other kind of business.

In this connection, however, it is proper to remark that banking in the United States is, in some respects, more hazardous than in England. Outside of the risk of loss through an over-certification of checks (as we spell the word) is the peril from irregular, forged, or fraudulent endorsements on checks payable "to order." The banker here is ultimately responsible, and is often mulcted when he has exercised all the care and caution consistent with the practical conduct of business. In England cheques (as they spell the word) payable "to order" are similar in effect to those payable "to bearer" in the United States. Bankers there are protected by the Bills of Exchange Act of 1882, which provides that

"When a bill, payable to order on demand, is drawn on a banker, and the banker on whom it is drawn pays the bill in good faith, and in the ordinary course of business, it is not incumbent on him to show that the endorsement of the payee or any subsequent endorsement was made by or under the authority of the person whose endorsement it purports to be, and the banker is deemed to have paid the bill in due course, although such endorsement has been forged or made without authority."

" Crossed cheques," as they are termed, in England are more nearly like our checks payable " to order." The " Crossed Cheques Act " of 1876 [1] describes this form of draft upon a bank as follows :

"Where a cheque bears across its face an addition of the words 'and company,' or any abbreviation thereof between two parallel transverse lines, or of two parallel transverse lines simply, and either with or without the words 'not negotiable,' that addition shall be deemed a crossing and the cheque shall be deemed to be *crossed generally*. Where a cheque bears across its face an addition of the name of a banker, either with or without the words 'not negotiable,' that addition shall be deemed a crossing and the cheque shall be deemed to be *crossed specially*, and to be crossed to that banker. Where a cheque is uncrossed, a lawful holder may cross it generally or specially. Where a cheque is crossed generally the banker on whom it is drawn shall not pay it otherwise than to a banker. Where a cheque is crossed specially, the banker on whom it is drawn shall not pay it otherwise than to the banker to whom it is crossed, or to his agent for collection. Any banker paying a cheque crossed generally otherwise than to a banker, or a cheque crossed specially otherwise than to the banker to whom the same shall be crossed, or his agent for collection, being a banker, shall be liable to the true owner of the

[1] 39 and 40, Victoria.

cheque for any loss he may sustain owing to the cheque having been so paid."

The object of crossing checks of course is to guard against their payment to improper persons, and if relief shall ultimately be given to American bankers from the hardships often incidental to the responsibilities which our laws fix upon them, some modification of the English idea may be introduced here. As stock-brokers often combine the function of banking and brokerage a consideration of the difference between the British and American banking systems in this respect, is not inappropriate.

The Stock Exchange of London, like those of New York, is a voluntary association, and it is governed by its own rules and regulations, in so far as they do not conflict with the law of the land. The Special Committee of the House of Commons, "On Loans to Foreign States," which made a voluminous report on the methods employed in introducing new loans on the British market, said with reference to the organization of the Stock Exchange, that "such a body can hardly be interfered with by Parliament without losing that freedom of self-government which is the very life and soul of the institution." The chairman of this committee was Mr. Lowe, a former Chancellor of the Exchequer, and among its members were the Solicitor-General, Sir Henry James, Sir Charles Russell, Mr. (now Sir) John Puleston, and men of that stamp. The Royal Commission to investigate the working of the Stock Exchange in 1877 advocated its incorporation " for the purpose of strengthening its hands and increasing its efficiency in the future." Though the report was signed by the whole Committee, which was composed of Lords Penzance and Blackburn, Baron Rothschild, H. H. Gibbs, previously Governor of the Bank of England, and others of equal distinction, a large minority signed it with a reservation as to this recommendation. They all agreed that "any external control which might be introduced by such a change, should be exercised with sparing hand. The existing body of rules and regulations have been formed with much care, and are the result of long experience, and the vigilant attention of a body of persons intimately acquainted with the needs and exigencies of the community for whom they have legislated. Any attempt to reduce these rules to the limits of the ordinary law of the land, or to abolish all checks and safeguards not to be found in that law would, in our opinion, be detrimental to the honest and efficient conduct of business."

CHAPTER VII.

PARIS—THE BOURSE; ITS ORIGIN AND GROWTH.

IT is tantalizing to an inquirer into the early history of financial and commercial institutions in France, even more than in England, to discover how little their origin is noted by contemporary chroniclers. History is rather a record of war and politics than of the victories of peace and industry. We learn that merchants assembled in Paris five hundred years ago, but this fact is mainly preserved by the name of the Bridge by the side of which they met—the *Pont-au-change*. Finally, in 1724, the business of stock brokerage had risen to such a dignity, owing to the enormous speculations in the Mississippi Company's shares, that the Bourse was legalized and assigned to the Hotel de Nevers, between Rue Vivienne and Rue Richelieu. On October 25, 1726, by an order of the Council of State, an official distinction was made between brokers in stocks and in merchandise. In 1786 that portion of the law of 1724 which granted the right to sixty persons to do the business of stock-brokers without payment to the state was repealed, and sixty officers (or brokers) were appointed for life upon the payment of a sum of money to the state. The Revolution swept away this monopoly in the law of 1791; but four years later, the free exercise of the right to do business as a stock-broker was prohibited, and twenty-five brokers were established. In 1801 the number was limited to eighty, but in 1816 it was again reduced to sixty, and this limitation as to number of official brokers exists to-day. M. Alph. Courtois, Fils,[1] says that in 1801 the security deposited with the government by each of the sixty *Agents de Change* was 60,000 francs, increased in 1805 to 100,000, in 1816 to 125,000, and finally, by the Imperial Decree of October 1, 1862, the sum was fixed at 250,000 francs for the Paris Bourse, 40,000 for Lyons, 30,000 for Marseilles, Bordeaux, etc. This last act still remains in force, and each of the sixty *Agents de Change* in Paris has lodged with the Minister of Finance 250,000 francs, which is liable for his obligations in the event of his default. He receives 3 per cent. from the government for his deposit, and while the

[1] *Opérations de Bourse et de Change.*

public have security in this pledge, it is not hazarding much to say that the government farmed out the exclusive rights in perpetuity to sixty persons as officially recognized brokers in Paris, in consideration of this deposit! It was impecuniosity and not statesmanship that devised the plan, and several times "raised the stakes."

The number of legally recognized brokers being limited, and the power to nominate a successor inhering in the office, it follows that the privilege of membership in this select body became very valuable. M. Courtois states that before the Revolution memberships commanded no price, that afterwards a sale was made at 30,000 francs, and that before 1830 they had increased to 850,000 francs. After the Revolution of July they fell to 250,000, rising to 950,000 francs before 1848. The Revolution in that year depreciated the value of memberships to 400,000 francs, but at present they command about 2,000,000 francs (or say $400,000).

A "seat" in the *Parquet* can only be obtained by purchase, and as many as twelve persons may be partners in its ownership, though it must be placed in the name, and under the control of some one of its proprietors, who alone has the right to do business in the Bourse, and who must own outright at least one fourth of the membership. He must not only be elected by his fellows after making the purchase of the seat, but his election must be confirmed by the Minister of Finance, who nominates him as one of the official *agents*, before he can exercise the duties of his office as broker. Members must furnish the Syndic annually with a list of their employés, stating what salaries they receive, and also permit the public exhibit of the names and interests of any partners they may have. The silent partners are personally liable for all the obligations incurred by the active partner while acting in his capacity as *Agent de Change*.

No one can become an *Agent de Change* who is not a Frenchman, at least twenty-five years of age, recommended by several bankers and commercial houses. He is forbidden to speculate or do business on his own account. He must keep his books on the double-entry plan, after a model furnished by the Syndical Board, and he cannot bring an action in the courts without its authority. If he should be obliged to leave business, even temporarily, he must notify the Syndic of the fact, and who his representative will be during his absence.

With all the financial interests that are focused in the Bourse it is physically impossible for sixty persons to properly perform the functions devolving upon them. Moreover, to confer upon any body, however large, such autocratic power and privilege, would be regarded in this country as an abuse of constitutional right, and an act in restraint of trade.

The exclusive rights given to the *Agents de Change* led to the gradual growth of a body of unlicensed brokers called *Coulissiers*, who form what is still known as the *Coulisse*, as distinguished from the *Parquet*, the name given to the body of *Agents de Change*. The *Coulisse* began to crystallize at the end of the Napoleonic wars, and at first it confined its operations to French *rentes*.

The railway fever, beginning about 1836 and continuing ten years, was felt in France pretty much as in England, and in the latter part of that decade the shares of railway companies were literally spawned. From 1844 to 1847 the share capital of railway companies formed in France is estimated to have been over one thousand million francs (say $200,000,000). Forty years ago this sum looked much more formidable than at present, for since that time the floating capital of the world has been vastly augmented. Investments in railway securities, which were then experimental, are now the accepted outlet for the surplus capital of all commercial communities. There was naturally, at that period, an immense overflow of speculative business in these issues, and through it the *Coulisse* grew rapidly into a commanding position. Their number was unlimited and embraced, as at present, bankers, speculators, brokers, and investors, who either did not have the means, or could not gain admission into the restricted membership of the *Parquet*, as sixty places could not possibly accommodate the number of persons who wished to engage in this business. Finally the *Coulisse* had so poached upon the preserves of the *Parquet* that the latter body determined to assert their legal prerogatives, and in 1859 they brought suit against the *Coulissiers*. Twenty-six of the latter were fined 10,500 francs each for usurping functions exclusively belonging to the *Agents de Change*, and for the time being the *Coulisse* was dispersed.

Article 76 of the Commercial Code describes the privilege of the *Parquet* as follows: "The *Agents de Change*, constituted in the manner prescribed by law, alone have the right to negotiate public and other securities that may be quoted in the stock list, or to negotiate for account of others, drafts or bills or any other commercial paper, and to fix the rates therefor." This latter function has been allowed to lapse, and *Agents de Change* as a matter of fact never negotiate bills of exchange or commercial paper.

When the *Parquet* had thus asserted their monopoly they adopted a policy of semi-expansion by permitting authorized clerks to make contracts in cash in contra-distinction to transactions "on account," which latter in Paris, as in London, constitute the bulk of the business of the *Parquet*. Finally, however, the *Coulisse* reconstructed itself and the two divisions of the Bourse now dwell together in apparent harmony. The fact is, the *Parquet* feel that their tenure, like that of the House of Lords in England, is not so secure that they can afford to arrogate all the rights legally conceded to them. They feel bound to preserve their credit intact and to keep it above suspicion, for fear of losing their vested privileges. This was exhibited by their conduct during the great *Krach* in 1881, when the Union Generale failed. The *Parquet* had subscribed for shares in a new issue of stock by this institution, and had in turn sold considerable of it for future delivery to members of the *Coulisse*. Meanwhile the company suspended, and owing to irregularities in the issue the *Coulisse* declined to accept the stock tendered to them. The matter was carried to the courts, and the *Coulisse* won, involving the *Parquet* in immense losses, which almost bankrupted them. But they stood heroically together in mutual support, borrowed large sums of money upon the joint credit of the membership, maintained unsullied the credit of their organization, and doubtless thereby prevented an abrogation of their rights, which naturally might have followed any general insolvency.

CHAPTER VIII.

PARIS—THE BOURSE—PARQUET AND COULISSE.

THE Bourse occupies a stately building of free-stone, which, with its noble Corinthian columns and air of classic grace, might easily be mistaken for a church, public hall, or palace, and, indeed, its designation is the "Palais de la Bourse." When the city of Paris was constructing (1808–26) this temple of Mammon the grants were insufficient to secure its prompt completion, and the *Compagnie des Agents de Change* contributed voluntarily some two or three millions of francs towards its cost, and, in consequence of this act, a ministerial order was issued by the Treasury giving the *Compagnie* the free use of the building without charge. The spot where it is located is known as the "Place de la Bourse," and faces Rue Vivienne. The grand hall of the Bourse is open, airy, and capacious, and in every way a credit to the institution. Singularly enough, the Frenchmen, in spite of their reputed admiration for the fair

THE PARIS BOURSE.

sex, admit no women or children to the gallery. New York brokers, with their gallantry, would feel as if much of their sweetness were "lost on desert air" if they could not now and then pose to curious and surprised feminine visitors in the gallery. A Frenchman is as nervous as an electric eel, and the stock-market operates upon him like a voltaic pile. In a placid market he is like a jumping-jack; in a panic he deports himself like a victim of St. Vitus's dance. During the forenoon the Bourse is quite deserted, but at twelve o'clock, if one approaches it, he sees excited groups occupying every inch of space under the splendid portico, or peristyle. These are members of the *Coulisse*, and here is where they transact all their business in the daytime, except in French *rentes*, which, by courtesy of the *Parquet*, takes place in a corner of the main hall. When the observer mingles in the throng in this outer mart of the *Coulisse* he sees one group trading in Italian Funds, another in Russian, still another in Egyptian, again another in Panama Canal shares, and so on. These transactions are all for "the account," which means that, at the end of the month, when the "settlement day" arrives, the buyers will receive any stock due them, except French *rentes*, which are seldom delivered by the *Coulisse*, and contracts in which practically continue indefinitely, in most cases differences only being settled.

In the *Parquet* the settlement day in French *rentes* is also at the end of the month, but in other public funds, and in "values" (*valeurs*), as the French term commercial securities, the settlements are fortnightly, as in London. In both *Parquet* and *Coulisse* a clearing house performs functions similar to that in the Stock Exchange in London and the Consolidated Exchange of New York. In the *Parquet* the commissions are fixed at about $\frac{1}{8}$ per cent. each way, by the *Chambre Syndicale*, composed of a Syndic and six members, who constitute the governing body. The *Coulissiers* have no commission law, but usually charge about $\frac{1}{16}$ per cent. or half the rate charged by the *Agents de Change*, and they, too, are governed by a Syndical Board.

The *Coulisse* skim along on the surface of speculation, caring little for investment business, in which indeed they are handicapped by the rule of the French Treasury, the Bank of France, Credit Foncier, French railway companies, etc., which will not recognize any transfers of their registered or inscribed shares, except when contersigned by an *Agent de Change*.

The Bourse.

This is one of the perquisites of the monopoly enjoyed by the *Parquet*, but when necessary the *Coulisse* can always obtain this service by paying one of the *agents* his commission. As a rule, however, it may be said that the business of the *Coulisse* is chiefly speculative, and notwithstanding the fact that it is outside of government concessions, with seats of no value, because not limited in number and not transferable, it does almost as much business as the *Parquet*, and at times more. The big speculation in copper a year ago, for instance, was in the *Coulisse*, and there alone Panama Canal shares are dealt in. In the winter it pays the Credit Lyonnais fifty thousand francs for a large hall, where it holds evening sessions, known as the "Petite Bourse."

The *Agents de Change* stand around a circular railing (technically, *corbeille*), which in the Exchanges of this country is called either a "ring" or "the pit." Its diameter is small enough to permit each member to hear his *vis-à-vis*. Two small rings or spaces (*petites corbeilles*) are contiguous to the circle occupied by the select sixty. In one of the former, sixty clerks, one for each member, are engaged in making cash transactions on behalf of the *Agents*, and in the other the same number of clerks are occupied exclusively with transactions in the French funds "for the account" (*negotiations à terme sur la rente*). A third enclosure is set aside for persons who solicit business for the *Agents*. They are called *remisiers*, which might be rendered into the American equivalent of "drummers." The *Coulissiers* have no such a barrier as the *corbeille*, and consequently they form into a compact mass in each group, which makes the transaction of their business more laborious.

As previously said, dealings begin on the outer edge of the Bourse at 12 o'clock by the *Coulissiers*. At 12.30 the sixty *Agents de Change* assemble and continue dealing until 3 o'clock; whereas the *Coulisse* remains in session until 4 o'clock, not counting their nocturnal meetings. In Berlin the *Boerse* opens at 12, closing at 2.30 o'clock; in Vienna it is open from 10 to 11 and 12 to 1.45. Americans start earlier in the day (10 A.M.) than any other brokers, except the Viennese, and have a longer session (closing at 3) than any except the English. Each country, of course, has its own national holidays, in addition to those recognized everywhere, such as Christmas and New Year's. The

Parquet have an organization that perhaps more nearly resembles an unlimited partnership than any other Exchange. Their membership is so small that it is almost like a happy family, and their rules go so far as to provide that only one of their number may occupy offices in any given building, and in case of his removal none of his colleagues can open in that building within two years.

This leads to one of the peculiarities of Paris, which is the absence of any financial quarter. In London and New York brokers' offices and banks surround the Stock Exchanges, giving a distinct character to that part of these cities, so that the phrases " Lombard Street " and " Wall Street " imply banking and brokerage interests. In Paris, however, the " Place de la Bourse " is close to small and inferior shops, and nothing in its environment in any manner suggests the nature of the business transacted within its purlieus. Banking and brokerage houses are scattered all over Paris, but nowhere do they attract attention, because of their isolation. With all the speculative instincts of the Frenchman, with his love of excitement, his constitutional fondness for change in political life, his unceasing search for novelties, it is remarkable that dealings in American shares have never been successfully inaugurated there. Why the Bourse should maintain an active speculation in Russian, Turkish, and Egyptian funds, at the same time utterly neglecting American government bonds and railway shares, is a mystery. Some Parisians buy and sell "Americans," but they do so chiefly through London. The French people do not migrate much, and outside of the old "stand-bys" in foreign public funds and foreign enterprises managed by Frenchmen, their capital is equally domestic in its tastes. They will put money freely into a speculative experiment like the Panama Canal, because the rich profits arising from the investment in Suez inspire unlimited faith in their industrial Napoleon, De Lesseps, while they ignore the enormous speculative opportunities upon much safer foundations in the United States. Well-informed American engineers do not believe that the Panama enterprise can be successfully completed by the present company, and its possible bankruptcy may not only involve a serious financial crisis, but may also unsettle the foundations of the French Republic itself. The shares and debentures of the Panama Canal are held by retail shopkeepers, peasants, servants, and people of small means, and are avoided by capitalists, bankers, and shrewd speculators. De Lesseps has always appealed to the former classes, and as they were the principal subscribers and beneficiaries of the Suez investment, he now relies wholly upon them to enable him to complete his present undertaking.

Though the credit of France was so reduced in 1797 that 5 per cent. *rentes* sold as low as $6\frac{16}{100}$, and not higher than $36\frac{15}{100}$ in that year; though from 1816 to 1869 there was an annual deficit; though to-day its debt is the largest of any nation; and though it has passed through more internal vicissitudes than any other European commercial nation, it has never repudiated its obligations. In 1871, when France lay prostrate beneath the conqueror's heel and an indemnity of five milliards ($1,000,000,000) was required, the francs fairly leaped from the pockets of the loyal, frugal people, and the loan was subscribed for several times over. While the French are volcanic in their character and sometimes deluge their land with the lava and ashes of internecine war and external violence, they soon clear away the débris and go to work. They excel all nationalities in the arts of painting, design, cookery, and dress, and the world pays them a willing money tribute.

The Bank of France is the keystone of the arch of the public credit of that country, and it is one of the best managed financial institutions in any country. It has the sole right to issue currency, which it may do up to $700,000,000 value, stated in American money. In general the banking and credit system is less developed in France than in any other country of equal civilization, and the percentage of cash payments there is infinitely greater than elsewhere. Notwithstanding this, the Bourse is one of the finest examples of a perfected credit system to be found anywhere. In this respect it is superior to its commercial surroundings, but in its restricted membership and quasi-relations to the government it is sadly behind the times.

CHAPTER IX.

NEW YORK—EARLY HISTORY OF THE STOCK EXCHANGE.

TURNING now to America, it must be conceded that it was born of a speculative undertaking. The voyage of Columbus, over a mysterious and trackless ocean, was the boldest experiment, and in its results the most colossal speculation in the annals of human enterprise. In the language of the Exchange, Ferdinand and Isabella "put up as margin" the cost of fitting out the expedition, and their profit was the western hemisphere. The parallel goes further in this, that like many speculators they finally lost what they had gained. For the first one hundred and fifty years after its discovery the territory now known as the United States was hardly visited by Europeans, and the next one hundred and fifty years were dedicated to the establishment of a fringe of colonies along the Atlantic coast, and their final separation from parental authority. When the

Revolutionary War ended, commerce was in its infancy and capital scarce. After the battles of New Orleans and Waterloo the spirit of commercial and industrial life succeeded political and military ambition, and at this period in both Europe and America was inaugurated the era of the peaceful conquests of money and labor. The constructive idea supplanted the destructive.

Exchanges do not spring like Minerva from the brain of Jupiter, into full-fledged existence, but are the product of gradual evolution.

Though the New York Stock Exchange traces the germs of its existence to 1792, when twenty-four persons who called themselves "Brokers for the Purchase and Sale of Public Stock" signed a paper agreeing to charge not less than $\frac{1}{4}$ of one per cent. commission on such transactions, the real foundation of the present organization was not laid until 1817. In 1792 the public debt of the United States was only $17,993,000, whereas in 1816 it had mounted to $108,510,000, its highest sum prior to 1862. The year in which the Stock Exchange was ushered into existence as a regularly organized body with "a local habitation and a name," coincided with the maximum of public debt. Business was confined chiefly to private partnerships, and that, too, on a small scale, and hence the occupation of stock-brokers in those days was dependent almost wholly upon the volume of the national debt, except in so far as they might be employed in commercial paper, in bills of exchange, and the conversion of paper money into specie or the reverse. The public debt was gradually reduced, until 1835, when the President of the United States announced in his annual message that "all the remains of the public debt have been redeemed or money has been placed on deposit for this purpose." The rapid extinction of the public debt would likewise have almost extinguished the stock-brokerage fraternity had not the issue of stocks and bonds for railroad construction come along opportunely at this juncture, to furnish a worthy substitute for government bonds.

The "magnificent distances" in our country, and its boundless resources, opened a vista to the speculator which is not likely to occur again in the history of mankind. There lay on our Western border prairies and valleys as fair as the Garden of Hesperides and almost as primitive as the Garden of Eden. Beyond lay the mountains, locking in their stony embrace treasures richer than those of the island of Monte Cristo, and on the Pacific coast ran the Pactolian rivers of California. The speculator surveyed the scene, cast its tempting lineaments on the screen of the money market, and immediately speculative dollars chased each other in a race across the continent. The iron-horse invaded the wilderness, performing for the Great West what the "wooden horse" did for Troy,—it admitted the people who conquered the country. The railroad pioneered the way for population, not waiting for traffic, but anticipating its creation. In fact, capital discounted the future, and speculation, rather than investment, hastened the phenomenal development on the ever-retreating frontier.

The discovery of gold in California, supplemented by Australian gold and Nevada silver, enormously augmented the world's stock of bullion, stimulated the channels of trade throughout Christendom, and gave a new impulse to speculation. The panics of 1837, 1857, and 1873 momentarily inflicted great injury on private interests, but did not permanently retard the accumulation of wealth. As the country grew richer the proportion of floating to fixed capital increased, involving a corresponding enlargement of the vol-

Early History of the Stock Exchange. 71

ume of Stock-Exchange business. The Civil War, with the vast expansion of national debt, the suspension of specie payments, and introduction of a depreciated paper currency, all served to increase the fuel and fan the flame of speculation. The public debt amounted in 1866 to over $2,776,000,000, now reduced to $1,727,000,000, which is diminished almost every day by bond purchases. After the war railroad construction proceeded at an increasing rate, and the capital to-day actually invested in railroad property in the United States is estimated at about $8,000,-000,000.

Up to 1856 the laws did not protect stock-brokers in the right to recover money due from clients, but gradually legislation is emancipating itself from the narrow prejudices and antiquated precedents that used to put the stock-broker on a par with a "three-card monte" player. The statutes of the various States of the Union differ, of course, in their treatment of Stock-Exchange transactions but Legislatures and courts are coming each year to more clearly recognize the fact that buying and selling stocks and bonds on margin, for long or short account is as legitimate as buying or selling potatoes on credit. The absurdity that "a margin" given to a broker on a purchase of stocks implies gambling in a sense different from the margin of security given by the buyer of a house to the money-lender who loans upon his real estate, is dawning upon the intelligence of men who are sensible enough to be independent of the precedents of forms of jurisprudence which condemned witches. The broker now stands on a plane of legal and social equality with bankers, lawyers, and merchants, as the usefulness of his vocation justifies. Lawyers can afford to sympathize with the early status of brokers, because in the period following the Revolution in Massachusetts, for instance, as McMaster says[1] the feeling ran so high against the legal profession that lawyers " were denounced as banditti, as blood-suckers, as pickpockets, as wind-bags, as smooth-tongued rogues." Bankers will understand it, for in 1799, when there were only two banks in New York City, one of which was a branch of the Bank of the United States, the sentiment was so hostile to banking that Aaron Burr was only able to procure a charter for the Manhattan Company by subterfuge. Its banking privilege was concealed in an Act which ostensibly authorized the formation of a company to furnish the city with water.

[1] " History of the People of the United States."

CHAPTER X.

NEW YORK—THE STOCK EXCHANGE OF TO-DAY.

THE war and the expanding railway system developed the Stock Exchange, bringing it into a national and international prominence that it had never before enjoyed. The growth of this institution into its present commanding position has been within twenty-five years.

Up to 1865 the Stock Exchange was a nomad. From the button-wood tree in Wall Street in 1792 and the Tontine Coffee-House, on the corner of Wall and Water Streets to 47 Wall Street, thence to the corner of Wall and William in 1827, to Beaver Street in 1854, the Exchange finally made its way to its present habitat in 1865.

The building has since been several times enlarged, but it is not yet up to the requirements of an institution of its varied and enormous interests. It faces on New Street and Broad, with a wing on Wall Street. The main Board

Room is 141 feet by 145 in the widest and longest parts, with a ceiling varying from 62 to 80 feet in height, a gallery for spectators being located on the north and south side of the main hall, which has an area of 13,700 square feet.

The number of members has several times been extended, until it reached its present limit of 1,099, at an increasing cost of initiation, rising from $25.00 in 1823 to an average of $13,000, at which forty "seats" sold, in 1879. The present value of membership, or "seats" in Wall-Street vernacular, is about $25,000, which is $7,500 less than the price they sold at six years ago. "Seats" now can only be obtained by purchase from retiring members, as the Exchange has none for sale, and therefore their value fluctuates with the demand and supply.

There is a life insurance of $10,000 attached to each membership, and the insurance system is on the mutual plan of an assessment for each death. This has served as a model for other Exchanges which have adopted the same principle, but it is not a natural function and is in a measure inequitable. No person with any pronounced physical disability can become a member, which often works an injustice both to the applicant and the Exchange,

THE NEW YORK STOCK EXCHANGE, BROAD STREET.

as the man might be a very valuable acquisition from a business, if not from an insurance, point of view. This restriction subordinates considerations of finance to those of health, which is essentially wrong. Besides, within the limit of age permissible a young man pays equally as much as the older man, which is contrary to the law governing life-insurance policies. Those who wish to provide for their families could do so through the regular channels of life-insurance companies. The ten thousand dollars payable upon the death of a member do not go to his creditors, if he have any, but to such a beneficiary as he may select or may be in the line of direct inheritance. It would be more within the province of an Exchange to accumulate a reserve fund by contributions proportionate to transactions, to insure against losses from failures in the Exchange. The principal objections to this would be that such a tax would disclose the volume of each person's business, and that it would tend to the indulgence of weak brokers. There is no more reason why an Exchange should insure lives than why it should furnish coal to its members.

In 1864 the Gold Exchange was organized, and

from that time till the famous Black Friday in 1869 an immense speculation in gold was conducted; but the blowing and bursting of the bubble in that year destroyed outside speculation in gold. As the approaching resumption of specie payment robbed gold of its premium, the old Gold Room closed up in 1877, and its members went into the Stock Exchange, carrying with them the remnants of their business. The mania for speculation at this time in stocks and gold was so strong that business began on the curbstone just after breakfast, continuing "after hours" until dark, to be resumed again up-town in the Fifth Avenue Hotel at night. This irregular trading grew to be such an evil that it was finally suppressed by the down-town Exchanges.

In 1863 an opposition Stock Exchange, called the "Open Board of Brokers," arose and by popular methods and tireless energy it grew into a position of equality with the old body.

Henry Clews, in his recent work on "Twenty-Eight Years in Wall Street," thus alludes to the opposition "Open Board of Brokers":

"The membership began to increase rapidly, and business accumulated so fast, that the Board was soon enabled to take more capacious accommodations on Broad Street, contiguous to the Stock Exchange. In this menacing attitude the new Board began to make serious inroads on the business of the old one, almost one half of which it had acquired by the year 1869, when the old Board called a truce. It was seen by the judicious members of the Board that the competition was likely to work the ruin of both, and amicable negotiations were begun, which culminated in consolidation." When these conflicting institutions were united and the brains and capital of the street were concentrated in the reconstructed Stock Exchange, business grew to proportions hardly dreamed of previously.

Business in the Stock Exchange used to be conducted by congregating the members several times a day in the presence of the Chairman, who "called" one stock after another "on the list," and all those wishing to trade would do so on these "calls." Finally the business began to overflow into the intervals between the "calls," and this tendency to a continuous market became so pronounced that in 1875 the Stock Exchange abandoned "calls" on active stocks, only continuing those in bonds and unlisted securities, which, however, are more a matter of form than substance. The great bulk of the transactions are made as orders come into the market, without reference to the time of their receipt. In the Consolidated Exchange, business in stocks is conducted in precisely the same way. It has one "call" in miscellaneous and three "calls" in mining stocks, but they only cover a small portion of the business done in these specialties. The petroleum market in the Consolidated Exchange was for a time the largest in the country. It now does twice as much in this commodity as the Stock Exchange, but since the successful introduction of railway stocks into the Consolidated its members have lost so much interest in the petroleum market that it has become a "side-show." Pittsburgh, which is near the newer petroleum fields of Pennsylvania, at this writing is leading the New York, Oil City, and Bradford Exchanges in the magnitude of its operations in this commodity.

The Government of the Stock Exchange is vested in the President and Treasurer of the Exchange and a Governing Committee of forty members, who are divided into four classes. The first class hold office for one year, the second for two years, the third for three years, and the fourth for four years, so that rotation in office is secured by an annual election of ten members to the fourth class and to fill any vacancy in the other classes. The President, Treasurer, Secretary, Chairman, and Vice-Chairman of the Exchange are elected annually. The President's office is one of honor without emolument. His duties are not onerous, and are chiefly to preside over the deliberations of the general committee. He has power to call special meetings and *ad interim* to appoint special committees, but he cannot nominate the standing committees, who are appointed by the Governing Committee itself. The hard work of the Exchange is done by the Secretary, who is not only Secretary of the Exchange at large, but of all sub-committees. An immense amount of work of a complex character passes through his office, which is like the counting-rooms of a commercial establishment, and it is but proper that he should be, as he is, well paid for it. The incumbent, Mr. Ely, is a man of great force and excellent ability, and necessarily himself a member of the Exchange. The Secretary for General Purposes of the Stock Exchange of London is, in the same way, the factotum of that institution.

The rate of commissions and the mode of closing out defaulted contracts between members, the arbitration of disputes, the expulsion or suspension of offenders, are provided for by the rules of the association.

Before any securities can be admitted "to the list," the companies issuing them must conform to the conditions as to titles, form of certificates, etc., imposed by the Exchange. The Exchange in no way becomes responsible, however, for the real value of the properties. An "unlisted" department is also legalized with less restrictions than surround the regular list.

Purchases in the New York Stock Exchange are usually made "regular way," which is always understood, unless otherwise stipulated at the time a bid or offer is made. This means that the stock or bonds so purchased are deliverable to the buyer between 10 and 2.15 o'clock the next day. Since the Saturday-Half-Holiday law went into force in New York State, obliging the Exchanges to close up at midday, the Stock Exchange decided that the two hours of Saturday's business were too short to permit the delivery of Fridays sales, and hence all the business transacted on Friday and Saturday, except when for "cash," goes over till Monday.

Since an open offer to buy or sell means "regular way," a broker to "get the floor"

The Stock Exchange of To-Day. 81

(which is a right of precedence over his fellow-brokers) can offer his stock "buyer 3," or bid "seller 3." To sell stock "buyer 3" is to give the buyer the privilege of taking it on the day of purchase, or any one of the three following days, without interest; and likewise to sell it "seller 3" gives to the seller the privilege of delivering it on the day of purchase, or any one of the three following days, without interest. "Buyer 3" is a shade lower and "seller 3" a shade higher than "regular way" when the market is in a normal condition. If there is a great scarcity of stock, "seller 3" is lower, because the seller prefers to postpone the delivery, and consequently may be willing to sell it less than "regular way" to get the benefit of the postponed delivery; and so "buyer 3" may be higher when stock is scarce, because the buyer secures the right to procure the certificates on the day of purchase. These conditions are, however, exceptional. When certificates are very scarce for delivery, and it is difficult to rely upon borrowing them, a broker operating for a fall in values may sell "seller 10" (days), "seller 30," or "seller 60," which is the limit of time contracts. Stock may be delivered at the option of the seller on them at any time, after one day's notice to buyer within the time they run. When money is dear, or buyers are not in funds to purchase for prompt delivery, they occasionally buy "buyer 10" (days), "buyer 30," or "buyer 60." Such contracts give the buyer the right to demand the stock at any time within the period fixed in the contract, upon one day's notice. All time contracts for more than three days carry interest at the rate of 6 per cent., to be paid by the buyer.

The Stock Exchange of New York excels others in the accuracy of collecting full reports of transactions and rapidity in transmitting them to the public. Yankee ingenuity devised an instrument called the "ticker," which automatically prints abbreviated names of stocks, with their prices, on a narrow ribbon of paper, and the speed with which they are collected and published is a marvel. The quotations are obtained by employés of the Exchange, usually boys or young men, who stand in the various groups noting all transactions, which are immediately reported to telegraph offices on the floor. They are disseminated instantly by two companies, the Gold and Stock Telegraph Company, and the Commercial Telegram Company, which together let about one thousand instruments in New York City, at the rate of ten dollars per month. The former company was the original one, and it came into existence in 1867, but the clumsy instrument of that day has been superseded by various improvements until now perfection has been attained. This company is an adjunct of the Western Union, and the Commercial Telegram Company is a younger rival. Both pay a handsome sum annually to the Exchange for the privilege of distributing the quotations. The Stock Quotation Company performs the same service with equal success for the Consolidated Exchange of New York. Not only is the "ticker" service better here than in London, but the American plan is far superior to the English in furnishing first over these instruments, and later in the printed stock lists, the actual number of all shares and bonds dealt in, with their prices. A stock ticker in London gives such bidding and asking prices as may be obtained by the representatives of the Exchange Telegraph Company on the floor, but since the custom does not prevail there to make open bids and offers, a large part of the quiet business between brokers and dealers escapes the observation of the persons engaged in collecting quotations. American dealers hover

over, and intently watch the "ticker" as it rapidly unwinds the tangled web of financial fate. They are therefore amazed to think how it can be possible that immense speculations are carried on in Paris without a "ticker," though such is the case. Some years ago an attempt was made to introduce the system there, but the electricians in charge were inefficient, and the service was so bad that it was finally abandoned. The offices of the *Agents de Change* and *Coulissiers* are scattered throughout the city, and messengers and telephones are the media through which fluctuations are made known.

CHAPTER XI.

NEW YORK—THE COMMANDING INFLUENCE OF THE STOCK EXCHANGE.

THE flood-tide of speculation was in the years 1879–81, when business was much larger than at any time since, except during the "flurry" in December, 1886 when over a million shares changed hands in one day. The total number of shares dealt in on the Stock Exchange in 1881 was 117,078,167, against 85,-821,027 in 1887. In the earlier year London was nothing like so large a factor as recently, and the business then originated almost exclusively here.

"There were giants in those days "—W. H. Vanderbilt, Gould, Keene, Woerrishoffer, D. P. Morgan, C. J. Osborn, Henry N. Smith, D. O. Mills, "Joe" Mills, W. R. Travers, C. P. Huntington, Addison Cammack, and others.

Gould now is almost entirely out of general speculation, and devotes himself to the management of the group of properties bearing his generic name; the younger Vanderbilts are comfortable in their fortunes, with only a moderate speculative disposition; D. O. Mills is largely out of the speculative "swim"; D. P. Morgan, "Joe" Mills, Woerrishoffer, Osborn, Travers, and W. H. Vanderbilt are dead; Keene and H. N. Smith have lost their money, and at present there is a hiatus in the line of succession of heavy operators and manipulators.

J. Pierpont Morgan, of Messrs. Drexel, Morgan, & Co., is a great negotiator, with a more powerful command of capital than any other man in America. He makes important deals but is not a manipulator who distributes large speculative orders to swell the volume of business. The so-called "Ohio crowd," composed of such men as General Samuel Thomas, Calvin S. Brice, J. G. Moore, Jay O. Moss, J. H. Inman, and their Southern following, are equipped for speculative leadership if they care to exercise their talents. The "Rockefeller crowd" with Standard Oil money are valuable mainstays to the market when bargains are really offering. They are among the most solidly and commercially successful men who ever entered Wall Street. George J. Gould and "Eddie" Gould, as he is familiarly called, sons of Jay Gould, will inherit capital and a taste for speculation, but it usually happens that the boldest and most influential operators are those who have risen by their own individual exertions. The "Chicago crowd," with Philip D. Armour, Norman B. Ream, and N. S. Jones as leaders, divide their attention between breadstuffs and provisions in Chicago and railway stocks in New York. They are particularly accustomed to speculation in what are called the "Granger stocks," concerning which they have excellent means of information. They are dashing operators, and often attract a following by radical expressions of opinion. They are optimists and pessimists by turn, and really are very able and successful operators. B. P. Hutchinson, of Chicago, the king of Western speculators, has so far not undertaken any bold operations in stocks. Addison Cammack is the "Ursa Major" of the stock-market. He is not so powerful a factor as when his boon-companion, Woerrishoffer, led the way in campaigns that eclipsed any previous "bear" operations known in Wall Street. Mr. Cammack does not attempt to propagate his views, seeking rather to discover the moment for a natural reaction in a rising market for the purpose of attacking it by heavy "short" sales. If he mistakes the temper of speculation he is not apt to fight it.

Since it is easier to excite hopeful rather than despondent anticipations of the course of prices, it is much easier for a "bull" than a "bear" leader to inspire public support. The "bear" in some quarters is looked upon as a wrecker of other people's properties, which may sometimes be partially true if he resort to wicked falsehoods concerning them. But merely to detect the shadows which financial events cast before and operate upon this judgment is not essentially an injustice to any man. The "bull" may exaggerate the facts relating to a property in a manner equally as inimical to the public as the "bear" who predicts disaster. Predictions of trouble to come may avert its occurrence by timely warning.

There are a number of men in Wall Street, such as T. W. Pearsall, S. V. White, Russell Sage, W. E. Connor, A. E. Bateman, Frank Work, Brayton Ives, and Henry Villard, who are widely known in connection with its affairs. The Stock Exchange has a score of room-traders who, in the absence of any pronounced movement, can swing the pendulum of prices between the extremes of moderate weakness and moderate strength; but the great movements ever rest on intrinsic conditions, to which all alike must bend, and which the most remarkably successful men are the first to discern and press upon public attention. Great leaders will not resist the current, but go with it, pulling others along by force of their intellect and courage, allied, perhaps, with a personal magnetism which attaches men to their cause. The mass of securities has become so great that it takes an enormous influence or capital to do more than make an eddy in the stream of speculation, but young men with ability, ambition, and fresh blood are coming to the front and in time will no doubt supply the places left vacant by former Titanic operators.

The Stock Exchange to-day is the foremost exchange in the United States in point of wealth, ability, and extended connections. All the great banking houses and railroad stock operators are allied to it, and though some of its members are merely rich men's sons, and others are rather unprogressive, it is composed of men of the highest order of intelligence, sagacity, and integrity. Its members embrace some of the most gifted men in letters, politics, and society in this country. Wall Street men are proverbially generous, quick-witted, and liberal. They are not narrow-minded, and the mental vision of those who are successful extends to the remotest ends of the earth. They maintain the highest standard of honor, and agreements made between themselves in the confusing bedlam of excited markets are as faithfully observed as if surrounded by all the safeguards of written contracts.

There are, no doubt, in Wall Street, as elsewhere, many men whose smartness is but another name for rascality, and others whose saintliness cloaks contemptible hypocrisy, but when in their dealings they betray these vices they are branded with obloquy and driven from the street by the pressure of outraged opinion. The race for wealth is a fierce one, rivalry is intense, and the keenest minds in the country compete for the prizes, but the honest intention of fulfilling all contracts is the *sine qua non* of toleration in the financial tournament.

Though the trade of Wall Street is in money, it is very rarely seen there, as checks, bills of exchange, and credits perform all the functions of the real article. It is only in times of distrust that massive vaults fly open to expose their treasures of specie and currency: otherwise money in Wall Street is like faith, "the substance of things hoped for and the evidence of things not seen."

During the Civil War Wall-Street men were noted for their patriotism, and when Secretary Chase was in sore straits for funds to conduct the war at a very critical period, bankers and brokers in New York took the then discredited bonds of the government, and by their confidence set an example to capital, at home and abroad, that enabled the Treasury to market bonds which hitherto had no credit. All honor, then, to the Associated Banks and to the Stock Exchange of New York for their timely aid and assistance during the darkest days of the Rebellion!

Stock-Exchange men and bankers, as the representatives of values in all sections of the country, must necessarily take a deep interest in the prosperity and harmony of all. Those people who suspect the motives of Wall Street, especially when financial legislation is proposed, are victims of a silly prejudice. Finance is not a fixed science in all its aspects, but experience has taught many lessons which should be heeded to avoid unfortunate results, and those who study the phenomena of financial laws and customs should be accorded a friendly hearing by law-makers. The silver question, for instance, has within it the germs of serious mischief. The coinage of, say seventy-

five cents' worth of silver bullion into what the
fiat of law pronounces to be the equivalent of
a given number of grains of gold which pass
current throughout the world for one hundred
cents, is an arbitrary exercise of legislative
authority which is harmless just so long as the
equality of these two kinds of specie is not
brought to a test. So far the government,
while reserving the right to pay its obligations
in silver, has maintained gold redemption. If
any thing should occur, however, to cause a
drain of gold from this country, which speculators might artificially intensify, and the
Treasury should voluntarily or compulsorily
exercise its option of paying in silver, and if
that silver, by reason of a scarcity of gold,
were not exchangeable for it in the open money
market on equal terms by its recipient, who
had drawn it from the Treasury for export purposes, the country would at that moment be
precipitated into a panic. Gresham's law is inexorable, "a poorer drives out a better currency." On such topics as this the Stock
Exchange and banking interests of the country
should be listened to with a respect due to their
knowledge and experience.

The Stock Exchange of New York up to the

presént time has been essentially an American institution, for the securities dealt in are almost wholly domestic. Compared with the great foreign Exchanges it is provincial, but this naturally arises from the unexampled opportunities in this country for the employment of capital. When we have opened our mines, completely gridironed our territory with railways, brought all our farming lands under cultivation, and fully equipped our manufacturing industries, American capital will then migrate to foreign parts, and our Stock Exchanges will become a ready market for the shares, stocks, and debentures of remote regions. Money is becoming redundant in New York, and frequently, and for long periods, our interest rate is lower than in European centres, while the credit of our government is so high that the net interest obtainable on United States bonds is now lower than on British Consols or French *rentes*.

It will not be too much of a stretch of the imagination to conceive of the New York Stock Exchange dealing in the bonds of foreign governments before many years. In another direction its scope should expand, namely, in the shares of industrial enterprises. Hitherto the shares of transporting companies have occupied the field to the practical exclusion of those of manufacturing and producing companies. Here is a wide field for future growth. The American who contemplates his country's capacity to produce can hardly fail to anticipate that its triumphs in material greatness will eclipse the highest achievements of England, which is now the workshop, the banker, and the Clearing House for the world. There are more plums in the American than in the proverbially rich English pudding.

CHAPTER XII.

TECHNICAL TERMS OF STOCK EXCHANGES.

EVERY vocation has its characteristic words, phrases, and slang which dictionaries do not clearly define, and Wall Street business is no exception to the rule.

In the United States a "bull" is one who expects prices to go higher, and a "bear" is one who expects them to go lower. With us a "bull" or a "bear" may be so only in opinion, whence the adjectives "bullish" and "bearish"; whereas in England, when it is said that a person is a "bull of" a certain security, it implies that he owns it, or is "long of" it, in Wall-Street parlance. So when he is operating for a fall in prices, he is said to be a "bear of" the market, which with us is equivalent to the phrase, "short of" it. To buy one stock and sell another with the expectation that the one bought will advance and the one sold will decline, is a "hedge." The broker's charge for his services is called a "commission," which in the

New York Stock Exchange is one eighth of one per cent. each way on the par value of the security purchased or sold. A bid or an offer of securities in the New York Stock Exchange, when the amount wanted is not stated to the contrary, means one hundred shares of stock, or ten bonds of $1,000 each par value.

A "point" means one dollar on one hundred, or one per cent. on the par value of a stock or bond. This word sometimes also means a hint or a word of advice to buy or to sell a certain security, otherwise expressed by the word "tip."

"Stock privileges," as they are termed, are extensively dealt in abroad, and, previous to the Wall-Street panic of 1884, a great many of them were issued here. They proved to be an expensive luxury to their makers at that time, and were, moreover, discredited by the failure of one of the largest issuers of them. They are now far less popular and common, but something will always be done in them. They are commonly known as "puts and calls." A "put" is an agreement in the form of a written or a printed contract filled out to suit the case, whereby the signer of it agrees to accept upon one day's notice, except on the day of expiration, a certain

Technical Terms of Stock Exchanges. 97

number of shares of a given stock at a stipulated price. A "call" is the reverse of the "put," giving its owner the right to demand the stock under the same conditions. A "spread" is a combination of the two. A "straddle" is when the holder has the privilege of either "putting" or "calling" the stock, at the same price. This kind of business may be used as a means of speculation by persons of slender means who are willing to pay a few hundred dollars to some operator for the privilege of delivering a certain number of shares of stock at a price below the current market, or for the privilege of demanding the stock within a certain period at a price above that prevailing at the time. A "put" may also serve as an insurance to an investor against a radical decline in the value of stocks he owns, or a "call" may be purchased by a man of means whose property is not immediately available, but who may desire to be placed in a position to procure the shares at the "call" price, if they are not below that in the open market when he comes into funds. If, at the expiration of the time fixed in these privileges, there is no profit apparent to the purchaser of them, he simply allows them to lapse. The *marché à prime*, or market in "puts"

and "calls," is larger in Paris than elsewhere, and at the settlement period a time is set aside for holders to elect whether they will exercise the options which they have purchased. In fact, the proceedings of the *Agents de Change* are arrested for five minutes at that period for the *réponse des primes.*

A " margin " is the money placed by a client, the principal, in the hands of the broker, his agent, as a guaranty against loss to the broker. This is necessary, for a broker who goes into any of the Exchanges does not " give up " his principal's name, unless that principal happens to be a member of the same Exchange, and wishes it done. It therefore follows that neither of two brokers making a trade can be relieved from the fulfilment of the contract because his client failed to protect him. Thus, while commission brokers are really agents for others, in the Exchange they stand in the mutual relationship of principals to each other. The margin not only is necessary as a protection to them that their principals will not saddle losses upon them by being unable or indisposed to make good any differences incurred by the brokers on their account, but it is also necessary to assist the brokers in carrying stocks purchased. A margin is merely a partial payment, but a broker buying stock for a client on margin is compelled to wholly pay for the stock. If he lack funds to pay for this stock out of his own pocket he can borrow money from banks or money-lenders, pledging the stock as collateral security. Usually, however, he cannot obtain over 80 per cent. of its value from the money-lenders, so that if he has only a 10-per-cent. margin from his client, he must furnish the other 10 per cent. out of his own means. In Wall Street, brokers, as a rule, exact margins, which the English call "cover," at the time an order is received or executed; whereas, in London, this custom is less observed, and the element of credit enters more largely into their mode of conducting the business. Where the credit of the client in London is established, his broker does not, ordinarily, call on him for any cash until the arrival of the next "settlement day."

A "bear" who sells a stock "short" must deliver it to the buyer. In order that he may do so he must borrow the certificates from some holder, giving to the holder in exchange for the certificates their money value as indicated by the current quotations, to be returned upon the redelivery of the certificates. The object of the holder loaning his stock to the borrower is either to save some interest, or save putting up large margins on the stock with a money-lender. "Bears" rely on their ability always to procure certificates for delivery against their "short" sales, but it sometimes happens that so many actual owners demand their certificates simultaneously that the "bears" are only able to obtain the continued use of the certificates by paying a considerable bonus to the real owner. This is a "squeeze."

There have been in Wall Street several noted instances where a person or a clique purchased and contracted to receive more shares in a given company than were outstanding. When this concentrated interest suddenly called on the "shorts" to return the borrowed certificates, the peril of their position was disclosed, and they found themselves at the mercy of the rightful owners of the stock, who were able, arbitrarily, to fix a price at which the "shorts" might buy certificates necessary to make their deliveries. This is a "corner." Happily it is of rare occurrence, and experience has demonstrated that it usually results to the ultimate disadvantage of those who engineered it. The reason for this is that any stock which invites a large "short" interest is generally not of the most valuable character, and the fact that it has just been "cornered," and is all owned by a set of speculators, causes dealers to avoid it. Thus the originators of the "corner" have left upon their hands a lot of non-marketable stock.

A "syndicate" is a party of capitalists who unite their means to accomplish some financial object, such as the purchase of a property, a public loan, an issue of bonds or stocks, the reorganization of a company, consolidation of interests, etc.

A "pool," in the vocabulary of the Exchange, is similar to a syndicate, in so far as it means placing the funds of individuals in a common undertaking for a common purpose, but it flavors more of the speculative idea. A "pool" is usually an agreement among a coterie of operators to buy or sell a certain security and manipulate it. It may be either a bull or bear pool. A "bob-tailed pool" is a small one, by which a few operators, acting in concert, but with little cash, try to make a turn in the market. A "blind pool" is one in which the capital contributed is put in by different persons, to be managed by one who buys and sells at his own pleasure, without consultation with or giving information to his associates in interest.

A "boom," and a "panic" are the Scylla and Charybdis of speculation. The former is an expansion of credit and an inflation of value to an inordinate degree. Visionary schemes are floated during such periods of fictitious prosperity. This high tension of speculation is often followed by a "panic" in stocks, which is an unreasonable fright among speculators and investors, leading to precipitate sales and a general collapse of credit and values. It is usually followed by a period of dulness and depression.

A "flurry" is a diminutive panic or a speculative gust that upsets prices for the moment, in some isolated market, or a single species of property, but does not extend to general values. Being sporadic it soon passes away without widespread damage.

"Kite-flying" is to do business on an unsafe principle and without adequate capital, while "ballooning" is to inflate prices to the proportions of a bubble or a point of insecurity.

A "flyer" is a small speculative venture made, often as much for amusement as for profit, by a person not accustomed to speculate much, who wishes to make a quick turn in the market.

A "lamb" is a person without financial information or knowledge of the ways of the Street, and therefore a ready victim of newspaper points and hearsay gossip about the market. He is, in the characteristic speech of a mining camp, what would be called a "tenderfoot."

A "new Tennessee" is the name applied to a new member, who is usually hazed by his fellow-members when he first ventures in the Board Room. Occasionally a stranger eludes the door-keeper and finds his way on the floor, from which he is usually hustled out in a very unceremonious, though good-natured, manner.

A "room trader" is a member of the Exchange who trades on his own account, either on a large or small scale. He is not an investor, but a speculator, who may operate for a fractional profit or loss, or may let his profits or losses run for several points. He necessarily possesses the faculty of getting in and out of the market suddenly, and of changing his views with great celerity. To succeed he must be gifted with the ability to catch the momentary drift of sentiment and values.

A "scalper" is a species of "room trader," who will either sell at the offering price or buy at the bidding price, with the intention of undoing the transaction or closing out at a very small loss or profit. He is not supposed to have any opinions as to what the future course of prices will be, and rarely ever goes home at night with any interest in the market.

The rules of the Exchanges of New York forbid trading after the Exchanges close, but in times of great financial excitement business overflows into the streets and hotel lobbies and is called trading "on the curb." In the Stock Exchange of London many brokers in American shares congregate in an open area to deal in "Americans" after the official close, often until as late as 7 or 8 o'clock in the evening, or as long as prices come in from New York. Those who are not members of any regular Exchange and make a business of selling "puts" and "calls," or unlisted securities, on the street, are called "curbstone brokers."

When a security is dealt in on two or more Exchanges, a class of brokers devote themselves to a business called "arbitrage," which is buying in one market and selling in another when variations permit it to be done with a chance of

Technical Terms of Stock Exchanges. 105

profit. This levels prices and establishes a parity of values between distant markets. These persons are called "arbitrageurs," a word invented for brokers' use by adding a German termination to the French word *arbitrage*.

A "wash" sale is a fictitious transaction made by two members of an Exchange, acting in collusion, for the purpose of swelling the volume of apparent business in a security, or by "washing" it up or down in the absence of any outside orders, to give a false impression of its strength or weakness. Members engaged in this reprehensible practice are subject to suspension. When a manipulator wishes to attract attention to a certain stock he often resorts to what are known as "Cross orders." This means a distribution of both buying and selling orders, in such a way that prices shall be either worked up or down without the manipulator losing or accumulating much of the security in question. It is a legitimate and bolder way of accomplishing what is undertaken by brokers who make "wash" sales.

Stocks sell "dividend on" between the time the dividend is declared and the day the books of the company close for transfer; after that they sell "ex-dividend," which means that the dividend does not go to the buyer. When a company's directors meet at the time a dividend is declarable, and they decide not to declare it, the company is said to "pass the dividend."

A "stop order" is an order given to buy or sell at the best price possible after a security reaches a certain price, either up or down as the case may be. It is usually given to stop a loss, whence its name; but it sometimes is used for the purpose of following up one's position in the market on a plan of averaging. An "open order" is good till countermanded, but in common usage is written "G. T. C.," which is as well understood as the abbreviations "C. O. D."

CHAPTER XIII.

NEW YORK—THE CONSOLIDATED STOCK AND PETROLEUM EXCHANGE—ITS ORIGIN AND GROWTH.

SAN FRANCISCO twelve to fifteen years ago was the scene of a remarkable mining speculation, which centred in the Stock Exchange of that city. Memberships in that institution at one time commanded about $40,000, and the public at large were crazed with the mania to buy mining shares. The extraordinary deposit of gold and silver in the Comstock lode, under Virginia City, Nevada, opened the eyes and stimulated the avarice of people who, as we have seen, are all alike in the passion for acquiring sudden wealth. The echo of this Western excitement was heard in the East, and the New York Mining Stock Exchange, with an initial membership of twenty-five men, was established in 1875. Upon the discovery of the treasures of Leadville and other Colorado districts, another Exchange, called the American Mining

Stock Exchange, was organized in 1880 by Californians, who found the interest of the public, in San Francisco, waning with the decadence of the Comstock. The New York Mining Stock Exchange grew in numbers and influence, being largely composed of members of the New York Stock Exchange, and the rivalry between it and the American Exchange was finally ended in 1880 by the dissolution of the latter, and the transfer of its principal remaining members into the New York Mining Stock Exchange.

Mining speculation in New York for a few years was active, and a very large proportion of business men were in some way interested in mining properties, but in the majority of instances the results were unsatisfactory, if not disastrous. The rapid decline in the popularity of mining stocks rendered it necessary for this Exchange to discover some new branch of business to occupy the energy and capital of its members. This was found in petroleum, which commodity possessed a great many elements to commend it to the favor of a speculative constituency. The old Petroleum Exchange, organized in 1877, in very humble quarters, increased its membership to six hundred, moving into

THE NEW YORK CONSOLIDATED STOCK EXCHANGE, BROADWAY.

more imposing rooms; a new Petroleum Exchange, partly a secession from the old, was created with a membership of five hundred, under the name of the National Petroleum Exchange; and about simultaneously with this, dealings in petroleum were inaugurated on the Mining Exchange, which then had four hundred and seventy members. Here we have by the year 1882 three Exchanges, relying chiefly for the employment of their members on petroleum speculation, which was manifestly an abnormal and transitory condition. Finally the National Exchange was consolidated with the Mining Exchange in June, 1883; in November one hundred picked men from an "Open Board" of brokers were attached, and in 1885 the joint organization absorbed the Petroleum Exchange.

The fusion of these various interests, with some additional issues of memberships, into one institution, then and since known as the Consolidated Stock and Petroleum Exchange, was like the union of disjointed railway lines into a single and compact system.

Prior to the final consolidation, the New York Petroleum Exchange and Stock Board and the New York Mining Stock and National Petroleum Exchange, as they were then called, had each undertaken to deal in the same railway stocks which were bought and sold on the New York Stock Exchange. This decision naturally led to action by the Stock Exchange prohibiting its members from remaining in and aiding and abetting either of these aspirants. When the consolidation was perfected, and the membership of 2,403, its present number, got into working order, a gradual growth in the volume of its transactions in railway shares began, which has continued to the present time.

Not satisfied with its inadequate quarters in Nos. 60 and 62 Broadway, the Exchange resolved to erect a new and commodious structure, having funds in its treasury ample to pay for it outright. Its present splendid building was begun in May, 1887, and completed in May, 1888. It covers 58, 60, and 62 Broadway, facing on Broadway, New Street, and Exchange Place. The Board Room is 132 feet in length and 90 feet in breadth in the longest and widest parts. The floor area is about 11,000 square feet, and better lighted and aired than the Stock Exchange.

While out of its own building, in a half-basement, dingy and cramped, it passed its critical stage, when its surroundings lent neither credit nor dignity to its reputation. During all this time it was sustained by an *esprit du corps* that has welded it together in the bonds of common interest. It stands with reference to the New York Stock Exchange somewhat in the same relations that the *Coulisse* does to the *Parquet* in the Paris Bourse. Both maintain parallel markets, with high-priced memberships in one against low-priced or no-priced seats in the other. Commissions in the *Coulisse* of Paris and in the Consolidated in New York are likewise customarily only half those in the older institutions.

Young men with limited capital, but with active habits, are common both to the *Coulisse* and the Consolidated. Both are more given to speculative shares than to investment securities, and both trade " for the account," with Clearing-House arrangements and deliveries of only the balance of stocks after the period of counter-transactions, which covers one week in New York and two weeks in Paris. As compared with transactions in other kinds of business, a delivery of securities on the day following their purchase, is needlessly hurried. The Consolidated Exchange compromised between the plan of daily deliveries on the other American Exchanges and the fortnightly deliveries in the European markets. The Consolidated Exchange has a limited and incomplete bond market; its business chiefly runs into speculative railway shares, petroleum, and mining stocks. Its success in establishing an ample market in railway shares may be measured by the fact that the volume of its transactions in some active stocks equals and occasionally exceeds those of the Stock Exchange, and its aggregate sales of the entire list are from fifty to sixty per cent. as large. The business in stocks on the Consolidated Exchange is from two to three times the proportions of the combined transactions of the Boston, Philadelphia, and Baltimore Stock Exchanges.

It is true that it is not so independent and original a market as the Stock Exchange of New York, and also that it is influenced by the operations of the latter, which really fix the value of railroad property in the United States.

The characteristics of the Consolidated which have aided its growth are free trade in commissions, trading "for the account," a Clearing House, open relations with the public, who can get nearer to their brokers than in any other Exchange, and admirable management.

The Consolidated Exchange confers large authority upon its President, who receives a salary. Mr. Wilson, who has occupied this post for several years, has contributed largely to the success of the institution by prudent, diplomatic, and energetic action. A Governing Committee of forty-two corresponds to such bodies in all other Exchanges.

The Consolidated Exchange has a large Gratuity Fund, and it pays eight thousand dollars upon the death of each member, the money being obtained by a per capita assessment of four dollars.

CHAPTER XIV.

NEW YORK—METHODS OF BUSINESS ON THE CONSOLIDATED EXCHANGE.

THE London and Paris stock Clearing-House system, as we have seen, is a distinct economy of capital and labor, but it has, in the eyes of American brokers, a fatal defect, pointed out in Chapter VII., viz., the inability to pair off and close outstanding contracts and call for margins to protect them prior to the day of monthly or fortnightly settlement.

The Consolidated Exchange of New York boasts, with reason, of employing a superior system. Under the Consolidated plan, transactions made through the week must be closed on the Monday following, when a delivery is made to a broker of all stocks bought by him during the preceding week over and above all his sales of the same stock. While, in London, all his transactions would remain open for the entire "account" period, in the Consolidated Exchange, in New York, only such go over to the Monday settlement as have not been eliminated by counter transactions. The latter are paired off each day upon payment or receipt of the difference through the Clearing House on the following day. To illustrate: suppose a broker, on a Wednesday, should buy five hundred shares of Lake Shore at 104 and sell five hundred at 105, thus making five hundred dollars, he would put in the Clearing House that evening a sheet giving in detail the number of shares, prices, amount carried out, and names of brokers to whom he had sold and from whom he had bought, bringing down on this sheet figures showing shares even and dollars, five hundred, to his credit. This sheet, combined with all the other sheets in the hands of the Clearing-House clerks, enables them to bring together the ultimate buyers and sellers of that stock on that day, and out of some of them to receive the five hundred dollars made by this speculation. The Fourth National Bank of New York, which is the custodian of the money during the morning of clearance, will then pay to the broker five hundred dollars, which the Clearing House will certify is due him upon a balancing of that day's business.

Here we see the economy of avoiding the receipt of the five hundred shares which, perchance, he bought from five different brokers, involving, as it would, five checks of $10,400 each on his bank, and the delivery of the same shares to the five buyers, which would require five checks of $10,500 each from them. The Clearing House eliminates all this expense, trouble, and risk, and saves the bank from over-certification, and the expense of entering in their books the deposits and numerous checks.

If the broker had bought one hundred additional shares Lake Shore at 104, of which he remained "long," intending to take up the certificate the next Monday, he would have put in his sheet showing the above, and also that one hundred shares of Lake Shore were due to him at the common settling price fixed by the Clearing House for that stock on that day. If this price happened to be 104, he would receive from the Clearing House on the following morning an order on the Fourth National Bank for five hundred dollars, his profit on the purchase and sale first above referred to. He would not get the stock, of course, until the following Monday, but meantime some one would necessarily be apparently short of the one hundred shares, and the Clearing House would furnish him the name of some such person, unless he had himself found some one on the other side of the market to whom he had loaned it.

Provision is made that either has the privilege of calling up ten per cent. margin, with thirty minutes' grace to procure it, and with the penalty, in the default of the deposit of the required funds with the chairman of the Exchange or some trust company, of the defaulter being closed out "under the rule." This is the buying in of short stock or selling out of long stock by the chairman, who assembles the members present, selling at the highest bid or buying at the lowest offer, the number of shares in question. The person who supplies the chairman with the stock or takes it from him puts himself in place of the defaulter, at the difference in price. The defaulter is allowed twenty-four hours to meet his obligations, and failure to settle within that time involves his suspension. If he settles his debt later he must apply for re-election upon presenting proof of the discharge of his debt. If he fail to pay within a year his membership is sold, and its proceeds are applied pro rata among his creditors on the Exchange. The law cannot compel a division of the proceeds of his membership among outside creditors, until his debts within the Exchange are all satisfied.

This latter process of calling for margins and closing out defaulters is identical with the rule on the New York Stock Exchange.

A year ago or more the New York Stock Exchange introduced a Clearing House and a system of trading "for the account," but as it was not compulsory, and as it was impracticable to conduct cash and time trading on terms of equality, and as it did not receive generous support, it was shortly abandoned. Whether it adopts the time-contract principle, which, with the limitation of only a week's duration, permits traders to "turn around" in the market without tying up stocks too long, it is not hazarding much to say that the Stock Exchange is very sure finally to use the machinery of a Clearing House for daily settlements in active stocks. The one argument urged against it is that the operations of large houses might be disclosed to the Clearing House, but this is not tenable. What is openly done by their representatives on "the floor" is observed, and it would not betray the origin of such orders any more if their representatives cleared the stocks through a Clearing House, than if set-

Methods of Business on the Consolidated. 119

tled by them as at present by private manual delivery.

"The proof of the pudding is in the eating," and the London, Paris, and all the Continental Exchanges use the Clearing-House machinery and trading "for the account." One step in the direction indicated is the agreement entered into among about forty prominent houses of the New York Stock Exchange to clear all their transactions with each other through the Manhattan Trust Company. This principle is bound to prevail.

CHAPTER XV.

THE SO-CALLED BUCKET-SHOPS.

THE Stock and all other Exchanges of this country have a parasite in the so-called "bucket-shop" which covers the land with a speculative mildew. It has discredited the legitimate business of regularly constituted Exchanges in the eyes of people, especially in the smaller communities, who form their ideas of real market-places from the character of these gambling houses. No doubt many an innocent critic inveighs against Exchanges and their members, because he imagines the "bucket-shop" is a section of the Exchange, and a miniature brokerage office. This parasite is indigenous to the United States, and happily its ravages abroad are relatively light.

A broker, it matters not whether in stocks, grain, cotton, real estate, insurance, or shipping, is an agent. His interest and that of his principal are identical. In a Stock Exchange, for example, he meets other brokers, and through the collision of orders and opinions, arising from operations of speculators and investors, news and events, sympathy with the dealings in other Exchanges, etc., a series of prices is established. These quotations go to the "bucket-shop" keeper, who exhibits them to his speculative visitors. In effect he says to them: "The markets in the various Exchanges are in progress; they will fluctuate. If you wish to wager that they will go up, name the amount of money you will bet on this, and I will take it, limiting your possible loss to that sum. If you wish to do the reverse I am likewise willing. Put up the stakes with me, and give me a commission on the bet, and we will await the result." Here his interest is diametrically opposed to that of the "customer" and if he should happen to be a man of easy morals, the quotations and information furnished might be qualified to suit the case.

Betting on what the price of a stock will be when the persons making the bet do nothing except to guess what others through their negotiations will make it, is as unadulterated gambling as betting on which horse will win a race. When a client buys a stock through a broker, thinking that it will advance, as when he buys a cargo of flour because he thinks the wheat crop is short and that it will go higher, he takes his position commercially in the market, contributing by the act of his purchase to bring about the very result expected. He relieves somebody of the stock or the flour. When, however, he, as a third person, merely puts up his money on what other persons, solely and without his intervention in the article dealt in, will do, he is as far outside the pale of commerce as if he bets on the throw of dice. The Exchanges have tried to suppress "bucket-shops" by appeals to law and legislation, but, by some strange obliquity of mental vision, those who alone can give relief do not seem to see the vicious nature of this financial pest. There is hardly a town in the land but what has, or has had, a shop of this description. They are financial nomads, changing their firm names and habitat to suit their pecuniary exigencies. They belong to no association, are accountable to no authority, and the sums they owe confiding customers are generally too small to justify an appeal to law; besides, many patrons would not like to advertise their dealings.

The "bucket-shop" keeper exhibits to his visitors the current quotations of some regularly conducted Exchange, and if the patron of the shop thinks that the members of that Exchange will buy enough Western Union, for instance, to advance its price, he deposits, we will say, ten dollars with the cashier of the "bucket-shop," and "buys" ten shares of Western Union at 85 from its keeper, who stands ready either to buy or sell, on the latest quotations, at the pleasure of the patron. Here a margin of one per cent. is put up, and unless otherwise stipulated, if the stock in the market on which they are betting goes down to $84\frac{1}{4}$ or $84\frac{1}{8}$ (depending on the "commission" charged), the patron's margin is exhausted and the game closed.

Sometimes, if the standing of the patron is known, the "bucket-shop" keeper will let the loss run against the customer a point or so more, upon an agreement by the patron to "protect" the trade. If the market goes in his favor, he can "close out" the contracts when he chooses, and then the "bucket-shop" will owe him the margin originally deposited and the profit made.

There are thousands of these "bucket-shops" in the country, and many of them are in small towns where there is no legitimate speculative or investment business in stocks, and where no legitimate broker could bring quotations and thrive. In these places "bucket-shops" furnish the excitement and diversion of gaming houses in the larger cities, which would not be tolerated in smaller communities.

The keeper of them could not afford to hire a special wire to procure quotations from a distant Exchange, and he probably might not dare to assume the risks of " taking the trades " of his patrons. Bolder and more enterprising men often lease private wires between the larger cities, sub-let loops to way places, forward quotations over them, and in return expect the " orders " picked up by these retail offices. Some of these larger " bucket-shop " concerns are believed to have made money, partly by profits on leased wires, partly on commissions charged, and largely on the fact that the majority of small and poorly informed speculators lose money, which of course is a net gain to the "bucket-shop." It is betting against the " bank."

Unsophisticated " lambs " are usually willing to accept small profits, and let their losses run as long as they have ready money to protect their position, and it is this unfortunate method of speculation which enriches the "bucket-shop."

It cannot be expected that " bucket-shop "

keepers will give their patrons any valuable or disinterested information or advice, for the two parties stand in opposition to each other.

It is also believed that the larger "bucket-shops" sometimes employ brokers on the regular Exchanges to make sudden raids or rallies in certain stocks, at opportune times, to obliterate the margins of their patrons.

A "bucket-shop" business is a poor counterfeit of real Stock Exchange business, and it ought to be suppressed, as it is not conducted on legitimate commercial principles. It is a cancerous growth on a healthy body.

THE END.

www.ingramcontent.com/pod-product-compliance
Lightning Source LLC
Chambersburg PA
CBHW030357170426
43202CB00010B/1407